An Island in Istanbul

At Home on Heybeliada

by
M.A Whitten

Islander Editions
ADALI YAYINLARI

Publisher

Adalı Yayınları
Tel: 0216 382 52 80
Fax: 0216 382 52 90
www.adalar-istanbul.org

Text
M.A. Whitten

Series
Islander Editions
islandereditions@yahoo.com

Printed by
Sena Ofset
2.Matbaacılar Sitesi E Blok
4 NE 20 Topkapı-İstanbul
Tel: 0212-613 38 46

Cover Design
Metin Çağlayan

July 2006

ISBN 975-9119-05-6

In memory of my *abi*
John Macpherson
who also loved this island

Turkish Pronunciation

A Latin alphabet was adopted during the language reform of 1928. There is no q, w, or x in Turkish, and a few new letters were invented to accommodate Turkish sounds:

- *ç* = "ch" as in "child"
- *ğ* (soft g) is not pronounced, but lengthens the sound of the preceding vowel. *Yoğurt* is pronounced "yoh-uhrt."
- *ı* (undotted i) = a short u sound as at the end of "Anna"
- *ş* = "sh" as in "shoulder"

A few other Turkish letters differ from English:
- *ö* and *ü* have the same sounds as their counterparts in French or German
- *c* is pronounced like English "j" as in "jam"
- *j* is pronounced like the "s" in "treasure."

Words are written phonetically, even foreign borrowings: "cashmere," for example, is written *kaşmir*.

Author's Note

An Island in Istanbul: At Home on Heybeliada offers a view of Istanbul and the Turks as seen from a small island in the Sea of Marmara and through the eyes of a foreigner who has come to feel at home there. As Turkey inches along the road toward EU membership, it remains surprisingly unknown or misunderstood. Here the reader will find a glimpse into the fabric of everyday life in this beautiful setting: from friendship to dining to discovery of traditions and attitudes.

The first part of the book is the story of "getting there" via encounters with real estate agents, architects, workmen, bureaucrats and others along the way. The second part describes the many pleasures of finally "being there." Turkish political and economic affairs, fascinating though they may be, make only cameo appearances. Likewise, the exotic world of harems and *hamam*s is as rare in this book as it tends to be in any but the tourist's Istanbul of the 21st century.

It would not be possible to list all the Turks who have contributed to my appreciation of their country, nor to thank them adequately for their friendship and generosity. Some of them appear in this book. Some names have been changed; some have not. In a couple of cases, two people have been blended into one, and one person has become two.

I am grateful to Dilek Bıçakçı, Tom Delaney, and Cynthia Wolloch, who read and critiqued earlier versions of this book, and to Nancy Love, who gave encouragement when most needed. My husband, Ben, not only read and critiqued, but, more important, he shared these island experiences and friendships. Most of all, I am grateful to the people of Heybeliada for the *keyif* I have found on their island.

CONTENTS

PART I: GETTING THERE

PART II: BEING THERE

PART I:
GETTING THERE

I
AN ISLAND IN ISTANBUL

Not all those who wander are lost.

J.R.R. Tolkien, *The Fellowship of the Ring*

The storks have returned. On this small island in the Sea of Marmara, there is no surer sign of the change of season. Every spring and fall, they come…thousands of them settling briefly on Istanbul's Princes' Islands before continuing their twice-yearly migration. Istanbul's spring weather can be capricious, but we can always count on the storks.

In early May, they are the harbinger of the warmer weather and livelier days ahead, when the population of these islands swells with the summer crowds. In late August, as the temperature begins to drop, the storks come again, reminding us that the peace and solitude of the island's winter will soon return.

At first I didn't know about the storks. My seasonal markers were the bare, wintry gardens suddenly alive in April with lush wisteria, offering the first flush of spring color and hinting at the ubiquitous roses to follow in May. But, then, on one of the first warm days of the new season, under a clear evening sky, five of us climbed to the top of the island's highest hill, ready to share plenty of *rakı*, Turkey's anise-flavored national drink, and to soften its effect with oregano-dusted olives, spicy lentil and bulgur *köftes*, and the first green plums from the trees in our gardens. Our mission: to cast off winter's gloom and watch the sun set over the Istanbul skyline.

Settling into comfortable viewpoints at the summit, we were energized by the early evening breeze and the clear view of Istanbul, with Haghia Sophia and the Blue Mosque on the horizon. We toasted the sunset, the moonrise, the approaching summer, one another, and anything else that struck our fancies. Kaya, who moved to the island some years ago from the Black Sea town of Giresun, told stories of the hazelnut harvest season back home and vowed that we would all go there in September to gather the nuts by day and drink *rakı* together by night. Hatice, an overworked municipal official, was so caught up in the moment that she even turned off her relentlessly ringing cell phone. Aylin, now a successful New York businesswoman, spoke wistfully of her childhood on the island and of her regret that she would soon return to her life on that very different island, Manhattan. My husband, Ben, was keeping an eye on the *rakı* glasses, refilling them as needed.

Then from the right, we heard a rustling of leaves, and, suddenly, silently rising from below our hilltop perch, a mustering of storks, scores and scores of them, lifted themselves toward the sky. Their huge wings made only the slightest sound as they first swarmed, then flew in formation, looking as pink as flamingos against the rosy sunset sky. It was an awe-inspiring sight and left us as silent as the storks for what seemed a short eternity.

It was one of those moments no camera can capture, and seemed easily a match for the majestic silences of the Serengeti or, closer to my origins, the mysterious, creeping fog rolling in from the Pacific and spilling over the San Francisco hills. I wondered if there could be a more perfect moment: a soft evening, good friends, throats tingling from the fiery *rakı*, and the soothing serenity of this island within view of the clamor and chaos of one of the world's most magnificent cities: Istanbul. The unexpected bonus of the storks made me pause to reflect on our preposterous good luck in finding ourselves here. *Kısmet* works in mysterious ways.

Whether they really believe in it or not, Turks often talk about *kısmet,* the idea that certain things are meant to be, preordained, maybe written in a large, Allah-sized ledger somewhere. They use the word as we do, to mean fate. They use it, too, for a girl's marriage chances—"Has your daughter found her *kısmet* yet?"—as if there were only one person in the world for her to marry. Someone who usually has good luck or whose life is going well is called *kısmetli,* a word that might be translated as "blessed by *kısmet*" or just "lucky." But to avoid sounding too superstitious, Turks also have the saying, *"Kısmet doesn't come from heaven in a* basket." In other words, if you want good things to happen, you have to work at it.

Our first encounter with Turkey many years ago was nearly accidental, but maybe it was just *kısmet*. Our return years later was definitely intentional—no baskets from heaven. In fact, Ben and I lobbied hard to get the jobs that would bring us back. Our decision to live on an island in Istanbul eventually seemed as natural as breathing. *Kısmet?* Maybe. But Turkey—especially this island in Istanbul—is a place that grows on you. It enveloped us in a way we'd never experienced in the half-dozen other countries we'd lived in.

Our *kısmet*, if that's what it was, brought us to an island, Heybeliada, close to the heart of Istanbul. As the Bosphorus flows south from the Black Sea toward the Dardanelles and the Aegean Sea, it opens into the Sea of Marmara. Just as ancient geological movements carved out the Bosphorus, dividing Asia from Europe by water, those long-ago phenomena also created an archipelago of nine islands to the southeast of old Istanbul. Known as the Princes' Islands, they are administratively part of Istanbul, but spiritually in another world.

The islands are a place of serenity, far from the city's noise pollution. The natural beauty, clean air, and absence of motor vehicles provide relief to Istanbul's frazzled inhabitants. Populated for some 2,000 years, these islands have served as a serene spiritual retreat for medieval monks, as a place of exile for deposed or disgraced Byzantine royalty, and, since the late Ottoman Empire, as a summer home for Istanbul residents, particularly for Istanbul's non-Muslim "minorities" (Greeks, Jews, and Armenians). Today, the islands offer a haven in this sprawling city and a quiet life far from the din of traffic.

Heybeliada is a small and charming place that is often seen as no more than a weekend retreat or an anachronism. But to me it seems in many ways to be a microcosm of what is best about Istanbul or even about Turkey as a whole. Istanbul's major historical influences—Byzantine, Ottoman, Turkish, Western—have left their marks on Heybeliada. Today it is partly modern, partly suspended in time, still preserving the old-fashioned civility and gentility that are on the decline in much of Istanbul, but not depriving its residents of modern amenities like Internet cafes and imported bourbon. Most of the world has forgotten or never knew Istanbul's long history as a place of religious tolerance and ethnic harmony, but that legacy is still alive on Heybeliada and is an integral part of its history. The island, like Istanbul, like Turkey, is rediscovering and restoring its past while moving toward an uncertain future.

Heybeliada is a little world, but it has taught me a lot about Istanbul's history, the changes taking place today, and the trends shaping its future. Living on this small island so close to the large metropolis, I begin to gain a perspective that can too easily get smothered in the city.

If this was my *kısmet,* how did it come to be? Raised in California suburbs, I had no ties to this part of the world. Until my 20s I had scarcely been out of the San Francisco Bay Area. Nothing in my education would have drawn me here; there were no more than passing mentions in history classes of Anatolia, then called Asia Minor. I don't remember any mention at all of the Ottoman Empire or the Turkish republic or Mustafa Kemal Atatürk. My husband's experience was similar. Turkish friends are often puzzled and sometimes flattered that foreigners selected or even knew about this small piece of Istanbul history and geography. American friends mostly thought the idea of buying a house on Heybeliada was crazy, and our families saw this as just one more exasperating episode in a lifelong string of irrational decisions.

One of those was our decision, at the end of graduate school many years ago, to apply for teaching jobs only in countries touching the Mediterranean. "Professional suicide!" everyone warned. They were wrong.

That desire to spend some time in a Mediterranean country led us to Turkey, possibly the world's best-kept secret. When we accepted jobs at a university in Turkey's capital, Ankara, we knew next to nothing about the country. We found ourselves a good deal farther (several hundred kilometers) from the Mediterranean than we'd had in mind, but bus travel to the coast was cheap. It was an adventure and could just as easily have been some other place, but the Turkish university was the first to offer a job.

We traveled to Turkey that first time on a Turkish Maritime Lines ship from Marseille, stopping along the way in Genoa, Naples, and Piraeus. There were a few other young Americans on board. As they all began to disembark at Piraeus, they called to us to hurry. We called back that we were staying on until the end of the line: Istanbul. They looked stricken and simply shouted, "Why?" We gulped and confessed that we would be living there. Shaking their heads in disbelief, they hurried off the ship to begin their holiday in "safe" Greece. Had we made a terrible mistake?

The next day, as the ship approached Istanbul, we were completely seduced by the first sight of the famous skyline from the water. It is at least as dazzling as the approach to Venice by sea. Istanbul has grown and changed since that first view years ago, but the effect is the same. I can't imagine anyone first seeing Istanbul this way and not falling in love with it.

Before the activity of the city appears, the Sea of Marmara provides a gradual entry, with light playing on the water's ever-changing shades of green and blue, from aqua to indigo. The Marmara is a hybrid sea, sometimes reflecting the calm of the Mediterranean to the south, sometimes as rough and dark as the Black Sea to the north. From time to time, lively schools of dolphins can be seen making their way to or from the Bosphorus. In summer, large and small yachts dot the horizon. The silence is sometimes disturbed by a businesslike *hızlı feribot* (high-speed car ferry) humming toward Yalova or Bandırma on the far side of the Marmara.

At first, the Istanbul skyline is only an outline. As the entrance to the Bosphorus draws closer, the sea is filled with ships of all sizes waiting their turn to enter the narrow strait on their way to the Black Sea. Then, gradually, Istanbul's grandest monuments can be distinguished more clearly: the six minarets of the Blue Mosque; to its right, the Haghia Sophia, on this spot since the sixth century as church, mosque, and, since 1934, museum. The small dome to its right is Haghia Eirene, an exquisite Byzantine church that would be the major attraction in any other place, but here is dwarfed by its famous neighbors. Then, at the end of Sarayburnu (Seraglio Point) stretches the complex of the incomparable Topkapı Palace, high above Gülhane Park, an old Ottoman pleasure garden.

By now, the frenetic traffic on the Bosphorus is all around. Passenger ferries, car ferries, sea buses, fishing boats, tugs, pleasure boats, and the commercial traffic to the Black Sea all crisscross as they head toward their destinations. Each has its own sound, from the deep basso of the ferryboats and the persistent drone of the sea buses to the put-put of small fishing boats or the tooting of the tugs.

The layers of history begin to reveal themselves as other evocative names come to mind: there is Sirkeci Station, the terminus for the Orient Express. Across the way, on the Asian side, is Haydarpaşa railway station, historic gateway to the Asian continent. Near Haydarpaşa is a huge rectangular building with towers on the four corners: this is Selimiye Barracks, where, during the Crimean War, Florence Nightingale created the modern nursing profession. Looking back again at the European shore, there is the Golden Horn, separating Topkapı Palace from Pera, where the non-Muslim population of foreign merchants and diplomats lived in Ottoman times. On the hill rising toward Pera is Galata Tower, part of the 14th century Genoese fortifications.

In the old city surrounding the great monuments, there is a maze of narrow streets, colorful bazaars, ancient buildings in all states of repair from ruined to magnificent. Across the Golden Horn, along the streets leading up to the Galata Tower, are fine 19th and 20th buildings reflecting the wealth of the foreigners who built there. The area includes palazzos that served as embassies until the new republic required a move to Ankara. Up the Bosphorus, other Ottoman monuments are not quite visible, but today's modern Istanbul stretches into the distance: high-rise apartments and offices, five-star hotels, restaurants with panoramic views, shopping centers, and traffic jams to rival any in the world.

That first time, years ago, we focused so hard on the view of old Istanbul that we scarcely noticed the little islands nearby that would one day be our home. The adventure had begun, but at that time we thought no farther ahead than our two-year teaching assignment. We couldn't have known that those two years would be only the first sojourn in a long attachment to Turkey. But, of course, we had not yet set foot on Turkish soil and knew next to nothing about the place.

After that first experience, as we learned more about Turkey and found Turkish friends, we came again and again, sometimes just to visit, but several times to live and work, first as teachers, later as diplomats, then back to academia again. Each time, with each experience, it became clearer that Turkey, especially Istanbul, and most especially the Princes' Islands, would be a permanent part of our lives.

As we were preparing to leave Turkey again after one of these sojourns in the mid-1990s, it occurred to me that one way to make a place a permanent part of your life is to own property there. We'd missed the chance of doing that when we lived in France ten years earlier. Maybe we should consider doing it in Turkey. So, the decision to buy a house on an island in Istanbul began as something between a fantasy and a whim. Little did I know that the whim would soon turn into an instant decision. Friends once again thought we had gone crazy. But all those decisions were right and that has made all the difference.

******

Even a whim needs something to set it in motion. I was already thinking of retiring early, before the stress and pace of a demanding job took their toll and while I was young enough to enjoy the freedom. Since virtually all of my adult life has been overseas as teacher or diplomat, a foreign retirement seemed natural. A life spent in several countries has many rewards, but one drawback is the inability to put down roots in any one place. One ends up belonging everywhere and nowhere.

Living or retiring overseas is certainly not an original idea. Bookstore travel shelves bulge with volumes describing a foreigner's life abroad, usually in a picturesque village in Italy or France or Spain. I devour them all. For the space of a few hundred pages, I am part of a small wine-growing town or a mountain village. If the author's focus is the region's cuisine, I am heading for my kitchen before finishing the first chapter. But I always stop short of wanting to emulate the authors. I am of the Woody Allen school when it comes to bucolic settings: "Nature and I are two." I love peaceful settings and beautiful gardens, but I also crave the excitement and cultural offerings of a big city. Where, I wondered, are the peaceful retreats for those of us who are irretrievably urban?

Let's face it. An urban creature's desire for peace and quiet has its limits. Sometimes people learn this too late. The overtouted and increasingly overcrowded South of France has its appeal, but a friend who chose that option regretted it. He bought a charming old *mas* and spent a couple of years fixing it up. But once he'd gotten a good dose of serenity, his urban instincts kicked in and he longed for a lively performing arts center, plentiful cinemas, good restaurants, and well-stocked bookstores. He still travels from Seattle to his *mas* for a few weeks each year, but always takes along friends from home. He finds he has little in common with the villagers and becomes bored if he is there alone. No, village life didn't sound like us. Until we came to Heybeliada, we began to doubt the possibility of finding tranquility in the heart of a metropolis.

Our ever-skeptical friends and family were by now ready to accept the idea of our retiring overseas, but they assumed it would be in France: "You lived in Paris several years. You're a Francophile. France would make sense." Yes, but the lovely climate of the south is too far from Paris. And as sublime as Paris is, I like to be near a lot of water. A river doesn't do it. I need a sea. It's my early San Francisco training. Besides, I know the French too well to want to grow old among them. You need your full powers to deal with the French.

Other places might have been possible, but finally Heybeliada, a little island in Istanbul, was the answer. This might seem to be an unlikely place to look for a peaceful retreat. Throughout history—as Byzantium, Constantinople, or Istanbul—the city has been the bustling, boisterous crossroads between East and West. To many Western Europeans and Americans, Istanbul still seems impossibly exotic. Western European resistance to Turkey's candidacy for the European Union is a reflection of the lingering notion of Turks as the "other."

Perceptions are often slow to catch up with reality, and Turkey's image remains blighted by cultural blinders that can't see beyond harems, belly dancers, *hamam*s, and villagers in headscarves. The dynamism of the young people (most Turks are under twenty-five) and the stimulating intellectual and artistic climate in today's Istanbul remain little known.

But why Heybeliada? Ben and I first saw the island during that initial "professional suicide" teaching period. Ankara in those days, the 1970s, was a pleasant, but fairly dull place, and it is much too far inland for me. At every opportunity, we got on a bus and went to Istanbul for the sea and the excitement. On one of those visits, we took a trip to the islands…and never looked back.

The deep blue of the Sea of Marmara contrasts with the lush green of a pine forest covering more than half the island. The northern side of Heybeliada was still orchard land in those days, providing summer fruits and vegetables to Istanbul residents. Today's modern apartment buildings had not yet sprung up. There were mostly traditional, wooden villas, their gardens bursting with roses, fruit trees, and jasmine. The only form of transportation, other than foot or bicycle, was (and still is) the gaily decorated *fayton*, a wicker-framed horse carriage with bright colored cushions and *Oklahoma!*-style fringe on top.

The pace of life, even today, matches the transportation. No one hurries. Children can play in the street without watching for cars. Neighbors stop to chat. Walking along the peaceful island streets, visitor or resident can take the time to admire the colors of the bougainvillea and oleander, or the aromas of lavender and honeysuckle. There is an abundance of wild juniper, oregano, rosemary, as well as myrtle both wild and cultivated in private gardens. The island's only sounds are the clop-clop of the horses, the cry of seagulls and crows, the song of nightingales, the five-times-daily call of the *muezzin* from the mosque, and, on Sundays, the ringing of bells from the Greek Orthodox church in the main square.

In our earlier Ankara days, our modest teaching salaries precluded any thought of owning a home on Heybeliada or anywhere else. I wonder if I walked by my house at that time, admiring its "Victorian" style and inviting garden. If so, I don't remember.

Fast forward to the more recent past. We came back to Turkey, again to Ankara, in the early-to-mid '90s, this time as diplomats working with the U.S. Information Service, at that time the U.S. government's agency handling overseas cultural, educational, and media programs. When two jobs were announced in Ankara, we jumped at the chance to return. Unfortunately, these were far more demanding jobs than our earlier teaching assignments had been. We found little time for pleasure trips to Istanbul.

When, at last, my work took me there for several days, I carved out some time to see Heybeliada again. A Turkish friend mentioned that property on the islands had become surprisingly cheap. Why? Turks had become more affluent, and the Turkish lira was now convertible. Many who used to content themselves with an island rental in the summer were now traveling to France, Italy, or at least Turkey's Mediterranean coast. Many of the island's lovely wooden houses had fallen into disrepair; some had disappeared. Some, our friend thought, might be for sale. But my visit to Heybeliada wasn't really with the idea of buying. It was just a whim and a day's amusement.

II
COUP DE FOUDRE

Anyone who doubts the possibility of falling in love with a house—with all that implies of fast-beating heart, sweaty palms, and waiting for the phone to ring— just hasn't met the right one yet.

Marjorie Garber, *Sex and Real Estate: Why We Love Houses*

On a warm and cloudless Saturday morning in June, I went alone to Heybeliada, taking a seat on the rear deck of a crowded ferryboat at Sirkeci pier, just below Topkapı Palace. Along with the family groups, tourists, merchants, and students, I watched the Istanbul skyline recede as the ferry glided toward the islands—about an hour's journey. As the bridges disappeared from view and the monuments of old Stamboul grew smaller, it was time to move to the front deck for a better view of the islands as we approached. And also time to get to the business at hand. At Sirkeci, I had bought two of the dozen or more Turkish dailies at the news kiosk and now began to comb them for leads. One had a Saturday supplement for classified ads, including real estate, but there was nothing listed for the islands. The other had no ads at all, so I would have to improvise or trust to *kısmet*.

Looking up from the papers a while later, I saw the communication towers at the summit of the first island, Kınalı, looming up. Just beyond was the trio of other major islands, with Heybeliada in the middle. A few passengers disembarked at Kınalı, many more at the next island, Burgaz, the greener and more pleasant of the two.

In another ten minutes, we arrived at last at Heybeliada, where, along with scores of picnickers, I crossed the gangplanks thrown from the dock and walked along the pier to the seaside promenade. Taking a deep breath to steel myself for this possibly foolish errand, I immediately recognized the clean, fresh, and fragrant island air. It was like coming home to a place I'd never lived.

Just behind the seaside promenade is the business district of Heybeliada, a T-shaped formation of shop-lined streets. This seemed the best place to begin my search. Surprisingly, there turned out to be three *emlak* (real estate) offices on this small island, so I picked one at random, explaining to the *emlakçı* (real estate agent) that I was looking for something small, old, with character, but in reasonably good condition. Maybe an apartment in an old building. The *emlakçı* was a stout, unsmiling man probably in his late fifties. He sighed, put out his cigarette, grabbed some keys, and placed his tea glass under a framed sampler reading "What have you done for Allah today?" and headed wordlessly for the door, waving me along to follow him.

Still without a word, we arrived at a modern concrete apartment building. He tossed his head in the direction of the building, indicating we should go in. No, I told him, that's not at all what I had in mind. "We're here. Take a look," he urged. OK, why not? This went on three or four more times, walking up and down the island's hills under an increasingly hot sun.

This *emlakçı,* being neither young nor slim, was puffing hard by this time. When I showed no enthusiasm for the next modern concrete block, he scratched his chin stubble, shrugged, and said, "As a woman, you won't be able to make any decisions anyway. Come back sometime when your husband is with you." With that, he headed back down the hill.

The sampler in his office should have tipped me off. Turkey prides itself on being a Western, secular republic with equal rights for women, but there are still plenty of men who don't seem to have heard this eighty-year-old news. I wasn't going to let the remark discourage me, however, so I decided to return on Sunday and start over with someone else.

Sunday's weather was spectacular, so the boat was even more crowded than before. This time I spent the ferry ride looking more carefully at the sea, the islands, and the endless array of merchant ships, passenger ferries, yachts, and small fishing boats. Arriving on Heybeliada, I went by the other two *emlak* offices. The one on the main street was empty and locked, so I looked carefully at the third, a small office tucked on a side street between an electrician's shop and a shoe store. Before entering, I peeked through the window. There was little effort at décor, just a table, desk, and three chairs. Asleep at the desk was a slender young man without a beard or religious cap, so probably not too conservative to deal with a mere woman.

Yes, this *emlakçı* was my man. As I opened the door, he woke with a start and quickly rose to greet me and offer a chair. He even offered tea, as any proper Turk will do for a visitor. I went over the criteria again, but didn't mention the previous day's attempt. He thought for a moment, then assured me that he had just the thing. Encouraged, I quickly finished off my tea so we could head up the hill. As we approached the building, my heart sank. I'd already viewed that modern concrete block yesterday.

Maybe there aren't any old apartments, I thought. Let's try another tack.

"How about an old *house?*" I asked. "Maybe wooden, with character, good condition, but not too expensive. A view would be nice."

He nodded and took me to a *modern* wooden building. After an hour or so of this, he looked puzzled. He must have been thinking, "Surely this foreigner must want the newest, most modern. What's the problem? These are the best apartments on the island."

What he said, though, was, "You must have seen some of these yesterday." Of course he knew. On a small island, nothing goes unnoticed, especially not a foreign woman looking for a house to buy.

I thanked him and said, "Too bad. I would have thought there would be at least one nice wooden house for sale on the island." I don't know what it was that made the penny drop, but he brightened and said, "Oh, I know of two. Let's go look."

The first was indeed an old wooden house with lots of character and an exquisite carved ceiling. It was also about to collapse. By this time, I'd given up and wondered how soon I could get a ferry back to the city.

"Thank you," I said with a forced smile. "I don't want to take up more of your time. You've been very kind, but I guess today just isn't *kısmetli*."

"No, let's go see the last one. It's just around the corner," he insisted as he picked up his pace and headed for the corner. With no enthusiasm at all, I struggled to keep up with him in the now blazing sun.

As we turned the corner, there it was.

I knew immediately that I would live there. It was a wonderful piece of Ottoman history, a two-story house, gleaming white wood on the top floor and heavy stone below. A balcony jutted out toward the sea view, and a terraced garden lay alongside the house. Ever since my childhood, I have dreamed of living in a graceful, elegant wooden Victorian set in a garden. This was the San Francisco house I could never afford.

Ottoman architects, like those in San Francisco, were influenced by late 19th and early 20th century European style as they created beautiful wooden homes for clients rich and not so rich. There are far grander houses on Heybeliada, still more on the largest island, Büyükada. This house, the *emlakçı* suggested, might be called a *mini-köşk* (miniature villa). "Mini" in relation to some of the others, maybe, but the size seemed just right to me.

The house stands out immediately: most of the nearby buildings are soulless concrete blocks. Spotted around the island are other turn-of-the-20th-century wooden houses, some smaller, some much larger than this one. We took a moment to look at this house more carefully from the street.

This "*mini-köşk*" faces east across the Sea of Marmara toward the Asian side of Istanbul. Alongside the house is a three-level garden, terraced into the hillside. As I looked at the garden this first time, I saw an overgrown mass of green, interrupted by profusions of pink oleander and hydrangeas, roses of all shades and sizes, a huge bay tree, and a confused jungle of other barely identifiable plants. Three very mature grape vines covered a worn-out pergola on the upper terrace, and two others shaded the entrance path to the house. A retaining wall between the levels of the garden could hardly be seen through the vegetation, but the visible part looked well built and attractive. The few parts of the wall not covered by roses were on fire with brilliant orange trumpet flowers. This first glance also took in fruit trees and an unexpected palm tree looking as though it had seen better days.

I am not a gardener (that is Ben's department), but I have an urban romantic's response to untamed green spaces. I was completely charmed. Having no notion of what it would later take to get this garden into reasonable condition, I was ready to buy—and I hadn't yet stepped inside the gate, let alone the house. Although the garden had seen little care in recent years, some previous owner had loved this house and garden and lavished attention on it. There were enough traces to make the place enormously appealing. Grateful to my card-playing father for his lessons on keeping a poker face, I squinted indifferently at the house and said, "Oh, I don't know, but we're here, so we might as well look." The heavy iron gate was unlocked.

As we entered the garden and passed under a grape arbor shading the path, a smiling, middle-aged man hurried to meet us. I am taller than the average Turk and, as a gesture of hospitality, he produced garden clippers from his pocket, motioned for us to wait, and set about clearing away the low branches. When he had trimmed them to something a centimeter or two above my head, he gave a half-bow, grinned, and led us along the stone path through the garden to the stairs leading up to the front door.

I assumed he was the owner of the house, but when the *emlakçı* introduced me as a prospective buyer, he disappeared. He was the man of the house, but not the owner. His advice or opinion about the sale was unwanted. The deed was in his wife's name, a fairly common practice in Turkey; it is a way to ensure that a widow will have full title to her house. Otherwise, Turkish law, based on Swiss and Napoleonic codes, gives only part ownership to the widow, the rest to the children. The wife, Bingül ("1,000 roses"), explained that their children were grown and gone, and the house was now more than they needed for weekend or holiday visits.

My heart was racing as I tried to look as blasé as possible. Would the inside be as wonderful as the garden? As we stepped into the central hall, I knew this house was perfect. No, its bones were perfect. Its makeup was a disaster. My garden romanticism does not transfer to interiors. I like a tidy place. Because Bingül and her family used the house only on summer weekends, they had spent little time or money on maintenance during the twelve years they'd owned it.

Although the outside seemed to my untrained eye to have the look of a small Ottoman villa, the islanders call this a Greek house, or *Rum evi*. The word *Rum,* a corruption of "Rome," was the term used for Greeks living in Turkey. The usage goes back to Byzantine times when that empire was known as "the new Rome," but *Rum* was also used sometimes to refer to any non-Muslim. Heybeliada was mostly Greek, and this *Rum evi* is typical of the homes built in the early 20th century by Greek families, most of whom left the island during periods of emigration from Turkey to Greece (more on those later).

This was originally a single-family house and would have had, downstairs, a main entrance from the street, a reception area for visitors, a staircase from the ground floor entrance to the *piano nobile* (if I may use such a lofty term for such a modest house), and the more practical facilities such as kitchen and storage.

Upstairs, a *Rum evi* has a rectangular central room and four additional rooms, two opening from each of the hall's longer sides. This house had lost some of that classic pattern. A previous owner, looking for a little extra income, had removed the staircase and cobbled together a dank little apartment out of the ground floor space. The rental apartment was appalling, dark, and smelled of mildew, but some original features were still there and could be brought back to life.

This house's good bones were there, but they required x-ray vision. The central room upstairs opened on one side to a balconied living room and a bedroom facing the sea, but the owners' heavy draperies, intended to block the summer sun, obscured that view and cloaked the lovely moldings and large windows.

The central hall cried out for remodeling. An unsightly electrical fuse box dominated the wall. A partition across one end of the hall had only cheap plywood where once there would have been multicolored panes of glass. The area behind the partition was used as a small bedroom. On the back side of the central hall was a bedroom overlooking the rear terrace and, in place of a fourth room, a hallway leading to a kitchen and bathroom—both tiny, both less than basic—and then onto the terrace. Behind the house was a small building, presumably used by a gardener or watchman at some time in the past. The present owners used it for storage despite the mildewed walls.

This was just a quick walk-through, and the "makeup" problems were many, but even so I was smitten. It must be true that love is blind. After the tour through the house, Bingül invited us to the back terrace, where we sat under the grape arbor as she offered tea and cake.

Turks do not rush into whatever business is at hand. They inquire about health, family, activities, interests. If it is a new acquaintance, they take the time to establish a personal connection. Efforts are made to put the other person at ease, to see that the visitor is comfortable. It is one of the areas where Turks and Americans are the most unlike each other. An American is likely to want an all-business, let's-get-it-done approach, but Turks will feel uncomfortable if the civilities are not respected. Only slowly, after a glass of tea and a chance to learn something about the other person, are Turks ready to move on to the serious matter at hand. Once a personal relationship is established, obstacles begin to disappear. Without that personal connection, little will be accomplished.

That day in the garden on Heybeliada, Bingül seemed well named—as lovely and pleasant as 1,000 roses. She had the classic look of an affluent Istanbul matron: short, a bit overweight, nicely dressed, with perfectly coiffed blond-tinted hair and a hospitable manner. She seemed a charming, reasonable woman. That impression was to change in the coming weeks, but we were off to a good start.

As we sipped our tea from small gold-rimmed glasses, I wondered if enough get-acquainted time had elapsed and how long I should keep this fantasy going. Deciding that it was not too soon to move to the Big Question, I asked the price. The *emlakçı* named a figure that elicited an elbow from Bingül. She didn't know I could hear her whisper, "No, that was supposed to be our bottom price. Now they'll offer even less." To my amazement, the amount he quoted seemed quite reasonable and well within our means. I frowned slightly, and muttered something noncommittal. After the tour, tea, and cake, the *emlakçı* and I returned to his office.

"Well, what did you think?" he asked eagerly.

"Oh, I don't know," I lied. "My husband may be in Istanbul on business soon. If he has time, he might come to see it, but the price is much too high. It will have to come down a lot before we could even consider it."

I remember nothing of the return ferry ride. I was already mentally living in the house and making it beautiful again.

******

Back in Ankara, I happened to mention this adventure to an old friend, Esin, who said, "Ah, but my friend Ibrahim grew up on Heybeliada and knows everything about it. He can help you." Another basic lesson about doing business in Turkey is that everything—but everything—works on the basis of who knows whom. In many countries, if you want, say, to remodel the kitchen, you call several contractors, take bids, and decide which one is likely to do the best job at the best price. A Turk will think, "Which of my old schoolmates is a contractor or might know a good one?" We may join alumni organizations or even wear class rings, but we have nothing like the old school network of the Turks. At our first diplomatic posting, a few years after teaching in Ankara, we had a visit from a former student. He was now a Turkish businessman and needed some assistance from the Turkish Embassy during his stay. When he discovered that he and the Ambassador had graduated from the same private high school, he went to the embassy and sent in a business card annotated with the letters "GS" (short for Galatasaray High School) and a number (the year of his graduation). He was admitted to the Ambassador's office immediately.

It was quite normal, then, that Esin could not imagine trying to buy a house without a personal connection somewhere. Her friend Ibrahim was the perfect link. She insisted that we contact him. In fact, she phoned him as she spoke, and we were soon talking with a stranger who was to become one of our closest friends. Ibrahim, a retired Turkish Navy captain, graciously offered to help in any way he could. He told us he has many American friends and had spent several happy weeks in my hometown, San Francisco, on a naval training mission many years earlier. It was, he said, a pleasure to be of service to a new American friend.

I wouldn't be able to get to Istanbul again for some time, but by chance, Ben had a meeting to attend the next week. More *kısmet*? While in Istanbul, he went to the island with Ibrahim to look at the house and agreed it was meant to be. Ibrahim was in Ankara not long after, so I, too, was able to meet our new friend and benefactor. I liked him immediately. Ibrahim has an impish smile, expressive eyebrows, and a quiet sense of humor that peeks out frequently from behind the staid, gentlemanly demeanor expected of a Turkish naval officer. In his career and travels, he had acquired some fascinating stories to tell, along with a smattering of French to enhance his fluent English. He also turned out to have an uncanny ability to deal smoothly and easily with people of all types, from dignitaries to simple laborers. We were especially grateful for that during our house negotiations.

Ibrahim felt sure the house was solid, but he called an engineer friend to check it for structural weaknesses. There were none. We learned that Ibrahim grew up on Heybeliada and attended naval school there, and, it turned out, he had even lived in the downstairs apartment of this house for several months as a young naval officer. This had to be *kısmet*. Thus began several months of wrangling before the house was finally ours.

III
REAL ESTATE A LA TURCA

He who loves roses must endure their thorns.

Turkish proverb

Taking a short break in the midst of our island real estate venture, Ben and I were enjoying a weekend on the Aegean coast, settling into a bright and airy hotel room with a lovely sea view, when the telephone rang. It was Ibrahim.

"Bingül has changed her mind," he said. "She says she won't sell."

"What happened?" we asked incredulously.

"Once she had a buyer, Bingül's doubts began," Ibrahim explained. "She thinks maybe she agreed too quickly and sold too cheaply. She says she isn't sure she wants to sell at all. This is the only thing she owns in her name and she's nervous about giving that up. Once the money for the house is gone, she will own nothing at all."

"But we've already transferred the money to our Turkish account. Is there any way to change her mind?" we asked desperately.

"*Merak etmeyin.* Don't worry." he said. "I'll take care of it and call you back in a couple of days."

The bloom was off the rest of the weekend, but we had underestimated Ibrahim's ingenuity. As promised, two days later he called again.

"*Tamam.* Everything is OK now," he announced.

"How can it be? What did you do?" we asked.

"Simple. I told her this behavior was *ayıp*. These foreigners, who love our country and want to live here, have already sold their home in America and now will have nowhere to live."

Sold our home in America? What home? What was he talking about?

"*Gibi*, as if," he chuckled. "It might have been true."

An appeal to traditional Turkish courtesy to foreigners wouldn't have been enough to convince Bingül, but *ayıp* was the magic word. It means "shame" or "disgrace" and is a powerful word in Turkey. Bingül, who had gotten cold feet and wanted to keep her summer home, immediately felt ashamed that she would have her winter house *and* this house while we would have nothing. The deal was back on.

"Don't expect everything to be fast and easy," Ibrahim warned. "*Adım adım. S*tep by step. Everything will work out if you take it *adım adım.*"

The next hurdle was one we hadn't expected. A foreigner buying real estate in Turkey needs a release from the military authorities stating that the property has no strategic importance. It's a formality, but can move very, very slowly through the bureaucracy. Since our house is on an island, the Navy was the branch designated to give the release.

Once again Ibrahim came to the rescue. Despite our protests that it was too much to ask, he traveled to naval headquarters, some fifty miles away, and walked our papers through the necessary offices, greeting and drinking tea with old friends and colleagues. What might have taken weeks was accomplished in a morning. We were lulled into a false confidence about the rest of the process.

We assumed that the real estate agent would take care of all the paperwork involved in buying the house. In the United States, that's a large part of what the commission is for. On Heybeliada, as in the rest of Turkey, however, the *emlakçı* is often little more than a matchmaker. Once he had put us in touch with Bingül, his role was over until the closing, when he could collect his commission and give us the key. It seems this is pretty standard. Meanwhile, there were title searches and other legal details to see to. Our time was running short. Our jobs in Ankara were about to end. We had new jobs in Brussels, and our transfer date was approaching. We wouldn't be able to return for a visit until the next spring. It looked unlikely that the deal would be finished before our departure, so we needed someone reliable and knowledgeable to handle things in our absence. We needed a lawyer we could trust.

Kısmet was with us again. Fate had sent us Ibrahim, without whom the deal could not have progressed this far. We began to ask friends about lawyers. A Canadian journalist, who had recently bought a house in Istanbul, said he knew just the person. He arranged for us to meet Sevin, a lawyer who has a good track record of helping foreigners buy property in Turkey. He had the highest praise for her honesty and reliability, and was sure we would like her. He was right.

Sevin, a skilled and experienced lawyer, is of medium height, build, and complexion, but there is nothing average about her expressive eyes, keen mind, or flair for color (red is her favorite). She has the gracious manners of the traditional *Istanbullu* and, when dealing with a legal matter, she is completely focused on her work. But when office hours are over, she is equally dedicated to music, travel, and good food, especially the spicy dishes of Gaziantep, the southeastern city where her family has its roots. She shares her passions with her foreign clients, who nearly always become her friends. She hosts musical evenings at her home, invites friends to her summerhouse in Bodrum, and shares secret places she finds in Istanbul, such as unknown little restaurants or off-the-beaten-track designer outlet shops.

She made the legal process as streamlined as possible and acted as buffer whenever Bingül got restive—which turned out to be fairly often. Sevin, like Ibrahim, has become a close friend, but our first meetings with her were focused on buying the house on Heybeliada. We had no idea what we were getting ourselves into.

"Permission for a foreigner to buy a house in Turkey is not a problem," she assured us. "The basic rule is reciprocity. If a Turk can buy property in your country, you can buy property in Turkey. But that's where the easy part ends. Title can be complex—some of these houses have been around through changes of empire. Many buildings in Istanbul are nearly impossible to buy—the title may list multiple owners including family members long since gone to

Greece or Israel or, in the case of Turks, to Germany. Tracing them would be nearly impossible."

Difficult, yes, but it can be done. A Turkish friend, determined to buy a lovely house on the Aegean Sea, doggedly found every one of the dozen listed owners, including two in Germany.

Kısmet was still with us. Bingül was the only owner. But, because of her hesitations, we had run out of time. There were other legal procedures to complete, and the closing papers to sign, but we had to start our new diplomatic assignments in Brussels. We needed to give Sevin power of attorney to finish the deal in our absence.

She prepared the papers and fixed a time for us to come to her office in Sultanahmet on Divanyolu ("the road of the Ottoman court"), once the imperial artery between Topkapı Palace and the Grand Bazaar. Today it is lined with restaurants, travel agents, souvenir shops, and other businesses catering to the masses of tourists who descend on this district to see the major museums and monuments. But Sultanahmet is also the center for the city's law courts, and many lawyers have offices along Divanyolu, though a tourist is unlikely to notice them.

I have long had a love-hate relationship with Sultanahmet. On the day of our appointment, as so often in the past, I was awestruck by the majesty of the famous monuments—Topkapı Palace, the Blue Mosque, Haghia Sophia, to name only the top three. But any chance of becoming lost in meditation about Istanbul's glorious past was quickly shattered.

"*Alo. Güten tag.* Hello! The Blue Mosque is this way. Shall I show you?"

The heavy tourist traffic around Sultanahmet brings out hawkers and touts who spot foreigners and badger them to buy whatever they're selling. What will be this one's gambit?

"Let me offer you a tea. Please be my guest. I know a place nearby."

Ah, yes, it's the cousin's carpet shop gambit. He offers the tea and takes you to his cousin, who will provide the tea but knows that most tourists will then feel a sense of obligation to look at "just one or two" carpets. In the right mood, I might banter back, but mostly it's a bore. And today we were trying to move quickly to Sevin's office. We continued on our way, with zigzags and dodges to avoid the other touts along the way. It is a pity that these are sometimes the only Turks a visitor will meet.

Once inside Sevin's office building, we found a very different side of Sultanahmet. Between a *hazır yemek* (prepared dishes on a steam table) restaurant and a shop offering film, postcards, and tourist souvenirs, a wide hallway leads to the main business of the building: legal services. The ground floor has a bookseller specializing in legal texts, a *çaycı* whose only mission is delivering tea to the lawyers' offices, a photocopy service, and a practical shop or two for light bulbs or stationery supplies. A couple of years ago an Internet café made its appearance. Notary and other services are on the upper floors in the building, along with the law offices.

A small elevator took us to the third floor, where we followed a cheerless, mustard-colored corridor, devoid of décor other than opaque glass doors with lawyers' names and room numbers. Sevin's law office, at the end of the hall, is a suite of three rooms—hers, her law partner's, and a central reception room. As in any Turkish office, the first order of business was to send out for tea, which arrived minutes later, announced by the tinkle of tea glasses on the *çaycı*'s tray. Meanwhile, Sevin's receptionist looked through a jumble of folders to find the appropriate file.

There are fancy corporate law offices in Istanbul, but Sevin's is more typical of the independent lawyer working with middle-class individuals. Hers is more inviting than most other offices in the building. She has added a carpet or two, a few personal items such as her framed law license, a radio, and various knickknacks, vases, and ashtrays. She has tried to liven up the space with a painting of Leander's Tower and a still life done by a friend. As a quiet statement of her personal views, Sevin has also added a framed facsimile of the Magna Carta, reflecting her respect for the British legal tradition, and a photo of Atatürk, the revered founder of the secular Turkish republic. As evidence of her care in making a good impression at her court appearances, a round mirror on the far wall allows her to check her hair and makeup as she departs for the law courts.

Like the other lawyers in this building, Sevin keeps old-fashioned, almost Dickensian records. She recently bought a computer, but it is used mainly for e-mail and only occasionally for other purposes. Legal papers are kept in large cardboard folders or plastic sleeves. Each new item related to a client is inserted in the front, keeping a fairly chronological order to the contents. It seems to work.

Unlike the stereotypical lawyer, Sevin tries to hold her clients' expenses to the minimum. She has never heard of a clock ticking away expensive "billable" minutes.

"To do this power of attorney, we need services from several people in the building," she thought out loud. "Notary, photocopy, translation, interpreter. Let's see what we can do to save you some money."

She looked over the papers again and turned to Ben.

"How's your Turkish?" she asked.

"Not too good, but I can understand a lot."

Sevin recognized these as the universal words of someone with only minimal competence in a language.

"OK," she said, "The official interpreter is expensive, so let's try to avoid using him. Pretend to speak Turkish. Or, better, don't say anything. If you have to answer, look at me. I'll signal whether to say *evet* ('yes') or *hayır* ('no')."

We needed a translation of our U.S. passports, but there would be no cost to us; she had worked out some sort of barter with the document translator. There were multiple forms to fill out and sign, and the notary fees were unavoidable. Without the notary's seal, the documents would be useless.

These small, barebones law offices depend on others for all auxiliary services—translations, photocopies, photographs (every transaction seems to require several passport-sized photos). Sevin took us from office to office, up and down the stairs in the sweltering summer heat. All we remember is filling out forms, peeling off liras, trying to keep up with Sevin as she moved quickly from desk to desk, office to office. She greeted and chatted with everyone. Quantities of stamps were attached to each document. We signed over them as instructed.

I speak Turkish, but the legal vocabulary and rapid-fire questions were hard to follow, so, like Ben, I simply smiled and answered *evet* or *hayır* as Sevin directed. It all seemed chaotic, but she got the business accomplished quickly. We soon had everything needed to give her power of attorney to represent us at the closing and take care of the final financial arrangements. We didn't realize at the time what that meant.

Mortgages were unknown in Turkey until only the last year or two. Buying a house meant full payment in cash. We knew we could count on Bingül to complicate this, too. We had opened a dollar account at a Turkish bank and transferred the full amount from our American savings account. A cashier's check or electronic transfer would be easy. But, no, Bingül didn't like that idea. What if she signed the sale papers and then the money wasn't transferred? What if the check bounced? A cashier's check was, to her, no better than any other, but, in a country where several banks have failed, maybe she had a point.

She wanted it in dollars and she wanted it in cash.

"And I want all $50 bills," she insisted. "No $100s. The newspapers say there are too many counterfeit $100 bills."

Sevin worked on her for days before Bingül grudgingly agreed to accept $100 bills. We now realized that Sevin would have to carry the entire amount, in cash, from the bank in central Istanbul to the closing at the Princes' Islands deed office on Büyükada. We had more than a few sleepless nights imagining everything that could happen to her along the way.

On the appointed day, Sevin took every precaution. She placed the money in a briefcase, attached it to her wrist, and added a flotation device, in case the ferryboat might sink. She went alone, but tried to look as inconspicuous and normal as anyone can look when carrying a floating briefcase stuffed with money and chained to her wrist.

She was fully prepared for Bingül to be a no-show, but everything went as planned. The real estate agent appeared and placed his signature in the appropriate places. Bingül refused to sign until she had spent a full thirty minutes counting and recounting the cash.

Much later, Sevin told us the story of the night before the closing. Around 9:00 p.m., Bingül phoned Sevin.

"I have changed my mind. I will not sell under these conditions."

"Which conditions do you mean?" Sevin asked patiently.

"The price is not enough. Well, I might sell, but the buyers will have to pay my share of the purchase tax and the whole commission to the agent. He hasn't done anything for me. Why should I pay him? Let them pay him."

Sevin groaned silently. The real estate agent hadn't done anything? Didn't he find her a buyer? He had done his job and was entitled to his commission. Sevin thought for a moment and took a calculated risk.

"I'm sorry," Sevin said evenly, "there is no more money in their account. There is no way to close this deal tomorrow if you insist on this. I will not ask them for more."

Sevin assumed that Bingül would back down and take what she could get. If she insisted on more, she might lose the deal altogether. But it wasn't quite that easy. Bingül, like many other Turks, firmly believes that "rich" is a synonym for "American."

"I'm sure they have more money. Give me their telephone number in Brussels. I'll call them and they will agree. We will just tell the real estate agent he'll get his money later."

Ever resourceful, Sevin was quick to come up with two ways to stop this nonsense. It involved a couple of little white lies, but even honest Sevin was ready for that.

"Unfortunately, my power of attorney is good only through tomorrow. If you delay the closing, the deal will be off."

That was Lie No. 1.

"But if you insist, here is their telephone number."

Lie No. 2: Sevin recited a telephone number, making it up as she went along. Bingül, happy at last, immediately hung up.

About an hour later, Sevin's phone rang again. It was, of course, Bingül.

"Something is wrong with their telephone," she complained. "I've tried and tried, but I can't get through. Well, I don't want to wait any longer, so I will see you tomorrow as planned."

Sevin smiled quietly to herself, wished Bingül good night, and hung up. The next day, the papers were signed and all official documents filed. Sevin sent the keys to us with a full report of the closing. At last, the deal was done, but an unexpected setback soon followed.

******

Once the Heybeliada house was ours, we could settle into our new jobs in Brussels and not worry about the house until the next spring. Many island houses, used only in summer, are simply closed up for the winter. There was no need to think about things like electricity or water accounts, phones, or other needs. All of that could wait. But what about insurance? We now had an investment in Turkey and wanted to be sure it was safely covered. U.S. companies won't insure overseas properties, so we had to find a Turkish insurer.

We asked several friends about insurers and found that none—not a single one—of our Turkish friends has insured the family home. Turks apparently leave these things to *kısmet*. The thinking goes something like this: "The house hasn't burned down yet; it probably won't; so why waste a lot of money on insurance that will probably never be needed? And if there is a major catastrophe—earthquake or forest fire—the insurance company will have so many claims it won't be able to cover all of them anyway." Many Turks own multiple properties. Real estate investment makes sense in a country where the stock market is still fairly new and banks have been known to fail. The one sure inflation beater has been real estate. But it seldom occurs to anyone to insure. Insurance companies exist, so there must be some homeowners who insure.

But we don't know any of them.

Our request to insure an old wooden house for its full value was greeted with suspicion. Since we were in Brussels, we asked Sevin to check with some of the larger insurance companies. The first two she contacted turned us down. "We don't insure old wooden houses," they said flatly. Panic began to set in. We weren't prepared to accept the *kismet* approach. An uninsured house was a sure way to sleepless nights.

Only the Turkish network system would solve the problem. We called a few friends to see who might have some *torpil* ("pull" or "influence") in the insurance industry. Luckily, one of Ibrahim's neighbors, Alper, has an old classmate who is now president of one of the larger insurance companies. A few days later Alper called to report.

"Normally, they won't insure old wooden houses," he said. "Most people don't want them; they want modern apartment buildings. So, they buy an old house on a good piece of land, insure it, then burn it down, collect the insurance, and build a new apartment building. The insurance companies have seen this happen too many times, so now won't insure them at all."

Panic set in again, but Alper continued, "I explained that you are foreigners who want to live in Turkey and love the house and won't burn it down. As a favor, my friend will make sure you get your insurance."

We were referred to Elif, one of the insurance agents, who had apparently been told to be sure we got complete coverage. Sevin made an appointment to see her that same week. Elif took her boss' directive at face value and prepared a policy covering the house for everything from earthquakes (good idea) to the possibility of an airplane crashing through the roof (we are on no flight paths that we know of). Though we are on a hill, we are insured against flood. Though we are on an island without automobiles, we are insured against damage from cars. The policy was prepared with a list of installment payment dates—one large payment up front, then a series of smaller payments. What about paying all at once? That seemed more convenient, at least until we could move back to Istanbul from Brussels.

When Sevin relayed our request, Elif was puzzled. Few people insure their homes, but absolutely no one pays the whole premium up front. With Turkey's high inflation rate at that time, installment payment ensured a declining cost. The liras in July would be worth far less than they were in January. By the end of the policy year, the dollar equivalent of the premium would be about half what it was at the beginning.

Sounds good? Yes, but it also means that the value indicated for the house has also decreased 50% in dollar terms. If you have a fire or other disaster early in the policy year, there's no problem. But if the loss occurs just before renewal, you collect only about half of the actual value because of inflation. Eventually, we were able to have the policy and payment quoted in dollars, but it took several years and multiple levels of authority to get that done. This was our first hint that we had entered the land of the *memur*—strictly speaking, the word for a civil servant, but the *memur* spirit can be found in the private sector, too.

—

IV
FLAILING THROUGH BYZANTIUM

Some civil servants are neither servants nor civil.
              Winston Churchill

Byzantium, the great empire centered in what is today Istanbul, gave us the word "byzantine," meaning complex, intricate, even a bit devious. There's a reason for that. The Byzantines passed one important thing along to the Ottomans, who, in turn, left this legacy to the modern Turkish republic: a genius for complicated administration. One of the most important lessons the foreigner learns is how to get along with the Turkish *memur* (civil servant).

A *memur* is not well paid, and often holds a fairly boring and repetitive job. The bright side is that the job is secure and the family can count on it for steady income. Competition for these jobs is fierce. There are more than 1.5 million applicants for the annual civil service entrance exam. At most 40,000 will be hired. It is said that *memur*s are happy twice: the day they get the job and the day they retire from it. Civil servants look forward to their early retirement option, but for years they faced rapid erosion of their fixed pension in Turkey's runaway inflation.

Many *memur*s see no good reason to smile or to chat during the workday. Answers to inquiries can be abrupt or unhelpful. Getting a useful answer depends on how you ask the question; don't expect anyone to volunteer the information you need. In one office, we watched someone quietly grease the palm of a *memur* whose response was not a smile of gratitude, but a quick look around to see if anyone was watching. We spoke with a longtime expatriate in Istanbul about how to deal with all the government offices on our list: residence permit, tax, electricity, water, telephone, etc.

"You can't escape the *memur*," he told us, "so you need to prepare. First, find a Turkish friend to go with you—someone who knows the ropes and understands the vocabulary used in official business. Don't imagine it's going to get done quickly. Set aside plenty of time."

Sounds like Ibrahim, I thought. *Adım adım.*

He continued. "Bring every document you have that is even remotely related to the subject, and always carry your passport, plenty of money, and a collection of passport-sized photos. Enter the building, take a deep breath, and then just go with it. There will be times when nothing seems to be happening. Don't worry. Your Turkish friend is taking care of it. Take tea whenever offered; it's a good sign they remember you're there. There will be a lot of going from window to window, signing forms, and answering questions. Stay with it. And buy that Turkish friend a nice dinner when you're finished."

Good advice. Not so long ago, that applied just about anywhere. Over the years in Turkey, we've had our share of long lines, seemingly arbitrary rules, or incomprehensible delays. But Turkey is changing, and one of the most welcome changes is the erosion of some of the traditional bureaucratic style.

One of the best examples is in the banking sector. There are dozens of banks in Turkey, with varying levels of public or private ownership. Alper, who had been our entrée to the insurance world, had this advice about banking: "The farther the bank is from government ownership, the more efficiently it works."

At the time we bought the house, there were two banks on Heybeliada: one a semi-official bank, the other private sector. A look inside was enough. The first had no customers and only one teller. The other was a branch of a leading private bank known for its sophisticated advertising and an enlightened management that has pioneered, over the years, such innovations as ATM machines, bank-sponsored cultural centers, and student loans. This branch was painted in the company's trademark lively colors, had slick and modern décor, and seemed to be humming. The choice was obvious.

Too often I have gone into a bureaucratic office without all the documents that turn out to be needed. I decided to do an initial inquiry. It might save time later. I took a number and primed myself with a few bank-type vocabulary words until my number was announced. I approached the young teller, whose nameplate introduced him as Orhan.

"I'd like to open an account."

"Fine."

"What do I need?"

"Money."

"Yes, but anything else?"

"Just money. Well, an ID, too. Do you want to do that now?"

Amazing. I had just gotten some cash. Why not strike? The process of opening the account was as simple as it would be in any U.S. bank. I was feeling *kısmetli*.

"I hear that it's possible to have electricity and water paid automatically from bank accounts. How can I set that up?"

"Simple. Just bring us a copy of your bill so we can get the right account number. Then it will be ready to go for your next bill."

"That's it?"

"That's it."

Let's go for more.

"How about an ATM card."

"Sure."

He turned to his computer for a moment, generated a document, and turned it around for me to sign. When I'd signed, he said,

"OK. You should receive the card and the PIN number in separate envelopes within ten days. If you want to change the PIN number let me know."

Orhan looked about twenty-five years old. He was young, taking for granted the changes in Turkish finance brought about by Prime Minister and later President Turgut Özal's reforms in the 1980s and 1990s. He would probably not believe that just a few years before, this ten-minute process would have taken two or three tries as well as considerable wear and tear on the nerves.

Turgut Özal transformed the Turkish economy. Before his administration, this was a country of export substitution, non-convertible currency, protectionism, and antiquated financial procedures. The joke among expatriates was: "Hey, we've got a couple of free days. Let's go try to change some dollars." Now there were two ATM machines on our little island.

After we became customers, Orhan took special interest in us. We may have been his only foreign clients. As we began to furnish the house, we needed plenty of cash. Many merchants on the island don't like credit cards—the fees cut into their slim profit margin. For some of them, it's also a way to avoid taxes; a cash transaction may never come to the taxman's attention. Whatever the reason to avoid credit cards, many of them will give an extra discount for cash. One Monday I went to the bank to withdraw several hundred dollars to pay for some furniture and other household purchases. On Tuesday I was back again to get cash for a trip to Ankara. Orhan scowled.

"What happened to all that money from yesterday? You should be more careful."

In the old Turkey, dollars were hard to come by. The lira was not convertible and Turks were under severe currency restrictions. Now the Turkish lira is completely convertible, but until recently it was subject to runaway inflation. The economic crisis of February 2001 caused a 50% drop in the lira-dollar exchange rate overnight. Those who deal in dollars came out all right—as prices rose, so did the exchange rate. Prices might double or triple in the stores, but in dollar terms the cost was the same. Most Turks of any means began to keep dollar and lira accounts. On payday, they transferred their entire salary into the dollar account, changing it back into liras little by little as needed. This made an enormous difference in buying power.

The speed of devaluation and inflation could be breathtaking. Prices for major purchases like cars and houses were often quoted in dollars or euros. The local communist party (yes, there still is one) made this a rallying cry: "Get rid of the dollar! Honor the Turkish lira and Turkish flag!"

I had a couple of $100 bills to change into liras. Remembering Bingül's concern about counterfeit $100s, I hoped there would be no problem with these. As Orhan was filling out the form, checking the bills for authenticity, and verifying the day's exchange rate, he made sounds of irritation and disgust. Uh oh, I thought, I've got a bad bill.

"Allah, Allah," Orhan said as he turned to me. "The lira has fallen by 300,000 since I last checked an hour ago."

Over a ten-year period, the lira-dollar exchange rate went from 30,000 to 1,600,000. By 2003, the Turkish lira was holding steady and the government began plans to revalue the lira, lopping off six zeros. On January 1, 2005, when the New Turkish Lira went into effect, it became easier for foreigners to deal with Turkish currency, but our days as billionaires were over forever.

Turkey's EU bid has a lot to do with the changes that have taken place in recent years, but much of the modernization would have happened anyway. When we first went to Ankara in the 1970s, none of our academic friends had a television or telephone and only one or two could afford a car. Today those same people have cable with scores of channels, cell phones, and at least one car per person. Life in Turkish cities today is much more like life in any U.S. or Western European city, but that has its good and bad sides, too. Much has been gained, but it is easy to feel nostalgia for the unhurried, simpler life.

I wouldn't want to give up today's ubiquitous ATM machines, but I still have fond memories of the man who opened our first bank account in pre-Özal Ankara. He wore sleeve suspenders and arm guards protecting his freshly starched shirt from the inkpads he used for his battery of rubber stamps. The stamps were arranged in precise order on a series of holders. At least eight of them, from various holders, seemed to be required for our document. Once he determined that all the needed information and signatures were there, he took a deep breath and launched into an unsmiling but unintentionally Chaplinesque ballet of stamping as he switched seamlessly from one holder to another, one stamp to another, one hand to another. I've never forgotten him.

If the modernity of Turkish private banks causes nostalgia for the old ways of the *memur,* don't despair. The ethos is still alive and well in many government offices clinging tenaciously to old-fashioned procedures. On the Princes' Islands, we found a refreshing hybrid and another reason for the islands' appeal. Procedures on the islands remain fairly low-tech, but the *memurs* are relaxed, helpful and friendly to a degree rarely seen in mainland officialdom.

Our initial experience with island *memurs* was when we had retired and needed to get residence permits. We had been sheltered from this experience when working with Turkish universities or the U.S. Government, indulgent employers who took care of all the formalities for us. We had never set foot in the imposing Emniyet Müdürlüğü (police headquarters) in the Aksaray district of old Istanbul. The good news was that a residence permit is easier to get than a work permit; the bad news was that we would have to get it ourselves.

By this time, we had met Hatice, director of public relations, special events, and a host of other projects for the island mayor's office. She seems to work twenty hours a day, maybe more in the height of the tourist season. When we sit with her in her office for tea and a chat, she usually has a stress-relieving cigarette in one hand and a telephone in the other. More often than not, her cell phone and another telephone or two are ringing at the same time. While simultaneously talking to us and to the person on the first phone, she calls out to colleagues about upcoming events. Hatice fields a constant stream of assignments ranging from journalists' queries to charity fund drives, from summer festival preparations to special requests from the mayor. Somehow she gets everything done. Despite her schedule, she insisted on coming with us to police headquarters. She wanted to make it as efficient and painless as possible. Hatice is more *melek* (angel) than *memur*.

Looking for the personal connection that would open doors for us in Aksaray, she took us first to Kaya, a friend on the island police force. A version of "small world" is the saying that there are really only two hundred people in the world and all the rest is done with mirrors. In Istanbul it could be true. Among longtime *Istanbullus*, everyone seems to know or be related to everyone else. All you have to do is find the right link. Hatice soon learned that the island police chief had once worked in the same office as the current director of the residence permit office. With that entrée, she called the director, established herself as a colleague of the island police chief, and announced that she would be bringing us to his office. She embroidered the truth a bit by telling him that we were distinguished new island residents who should be treated as VIPs.

When we got to police headquarters, we passed through the airport-like security checks and went up one flight of stairs to the residence permit office, noticing the long lines in front of the ground-floor photocopy and cashier's offices. Upstairs, it was a scene from one of the less severe circles of Dante's *Inferno*. There were scores of applicants clustered around several counters, each trying vainly to catch the attention of a *memur*. Many applicants seemed to be from the former Soviet Union, some were African, a few looked Western European. Some spoke Turkish or one of the related languages from Central Asia. Others were struggling to find a *memur* who could deal with them in English or some other language. Among them were a few Turks, officiously moving around stacks of documents and passports; these were presumably professional handlers hired to do mass processing for corporations or other organizations. They'll even take care of an individual's paperwork…for upwards of $1,500 per person. Behind the counters were a dozen or more *memurs* going about their business, paying only intermittent attention to the clamor around them.

Our hearts sank. We asked Hatice where we should begin. She looked witheringly at us and swept us directly into the office of the director, a middle-aged man with a definite air of authority. He greeted us warmly, offered us chairs, and asked what we would like to drink. While we waited for the tea to arrive, he chatted about the weather, about his friend the island police chief, and about his own memories of the islands. His desk was uncluttered by anything but an ashtray and a frequently ringing telephone. He made fairly constant use of the former while inspecting our passports.

After a few minutes, he was ready to proceed. He picked up the phone, punched in an extension number, and summoned a slender young *memur,* who got his instructions, asked us for our passports and photos, and disappeared. We continued to drink tea and chat with the director and Hatice, wondering when we were going to begin the process. Supplicants at the office door, asking for a signature on a document, interrupted the director from time to time, but he and Hatice seemed oblivious to our reason for being there. As we should have known, however, all was in order.

A little later, the young *memur* reappeared. He had, in the meantime, filled in all the necessary documents for us and needed only our signatures. It was only then that we were invited to come with him to give the papers directly to the principal *memur*.

Walking from the director's office through the pool of *memurs,* we got plenty of strange looks from the applicants on the other side of the counters, but tried to avoid eye contact. Hatice smiled and greeted every *memur* along the way before shaking hands with the head *memur*, who signed our papers and directed us to another desk for stamping and filing. The young *memur* then escorted us to the cashier to pay the fees and back to the director's office. After a final obligatory glass of tea, the director told us to call him in about a month, when our permanent residence permits should have arrived from Ankara.

That was it. We were finished. Instead of a frustrating morning of trying to figure out the procedures, we had been able to relax and drink tea. All thanks to Hatice and Kaya. As if this weren't enough, they continued, over the coming months, to check with us to see if we had any problems or questions as we settled in. Soon we were getting together for evenings at restaurants or for walks around the islands. When we were all together for the memorable spectacle of the migrating storks, I couldn't imagine anyone more appropriate to share it with.

******

Technology and streamlined systems are transforming the old *memur* system. When changes come, they happen quickly. When we return to police headquarters to renew our residence permits, it is possible that everything will have changed. But there is one entrenched tradition that will never change in this country: the sanctity of the *bayram*.

The Turkish republic is a secular state, and Turks bristle if a foreigner inadvertently refers to Turkey as "an Islamic republic" rather than "a secular republic with a majority Muslim population." Though some Westerners think that's the same thing, Turks will explain that it definitely is not. The system is not exactly like American separation of church and state, but the lines are strictly drawn. Even so, there is nothing more rigorously observed by both government and public than the long *kurban bayramı* holiday period.

Kurban bayramı is the religious feast recalling Abraham's willingness to sacrifice his son if God so willed. It is as important to

Muslims as Christmas and Easter are to Christians, but the similarities are few. Each is preceded by a period of fasting, but the rigorous Ramazan fast, one of the five pillars of Islam, is far more grueling than the mostly symbolic Advent and Lenten fasts. From sunrise to sunset, the devout Muslim avoids all food and drink (even water), and must even abstain from cigarettes—a true sacrifice for a population that inspired the Italian expression *fumare come un Turco* (we say someone smokes "like a chimney," they say "like a Turk"). Following a lunar calendar, the start of Ramazan moves eleven days each year, so the fasting can fall in any season. In winter, the short daylight hours make the regimen a bit less arduous, but a summer Ramazan can be exhausting. Immediately after Ramazan comes şeker ("sugar" or "candy") *bayramı*, when the end of the fast is celebrated with sweet gifts. About two months later comes *kurban bayramı* and another of the five Muslim duties: the *haj*, or pilgrimage to Mecca. Whatever the season, when the *bayram*s finally arrive after the month-long fast, everyone is ready for celebration.

The story of Abraham is commemorated with the pious deed of sacrificing a sheep, as Abraham did when his son was spared, and distributing the meat to the poor. The streets of Turkish cities, towns, and villages run with the blood of slaughtered animals on the first day of *kurban bayramı*. During the days leading up to the holiday, shepherds appear with sacrificial flocks, each animal marked with a bit of red paint to indicate its upcoming fate. They are a pitiful, bleating sight and seem to sense what's coming.

Once the ritual sacrifices have been accomplished, the holiday—for secular Turks or others not making the *haj*—becomes a time for family reunions, parties, and vacation travel. In Turkey, the *bayram* lasts at least a week, sometimes ten days, and whenever it comes, everything stops. The French devotion to their August holidays has nothing on the Turks and their *bayram*. Once when my head office in the United States needed something done during what I knew would be *bayram*, I explained that it would have to wait until the following week. The head office didn't believe me. "Don't be ridiculous," they said. "Countries don't just shut down for ten days." This one does.

Our first trip from Brussels back to Turkey after buying the house coincided with the *bayram*. I knew that nothing could be accomplished during the *bayram*, but I hadn't counted on the pre-*bayram* phenomenon. In the United States, we take Christmas pretty hard, but know we can shop until the last minute. Lots of services and stores are available even on Christmas Day, or at least through Christmas Eve. For a Turkish *bayram*, though, that's not the case.

Workmen start scheduling their jobs for "after the *bayram*." Students easily get extensions on their assignments until "after the *bayram*." Friends or business associates can't possibly make arrangements to see each other at a specific time; they'll talk again "after the *bayram*." When Ibrahim asked his gardener to come and help us clean out our overgrown garden, the man needed a good excuse to get out of this very tough job. First he said it was the wrong season to trim the plants. Then he said he had too much work at Ibrahim's. Next he claimed that his wife had rheumatism and needed him at home. Finally, he thought of the sure-fire way out: "*İnşallah*, God willing, I can do it after the *bayram*." This was a double whammy. Not only did "after the *bayram*" postpone the work, but "*inşallah*" was an extra hedge. He promised nothing, but only indicated he might come if it was God's will. Needless to say, he never showed up.

During that same pre-*bayram* visit, we had to change the electricity account to our name. We went to the office the afternoon before the *bayram*. The electric company *memur* could not believe his ears. "You want to do this now? But *bayram* starts tomorrow. You'll have to come back next week." What fools we were. The office was open, the *memur* was there, we had all the papers we needed, but of course nothing could be done until after the *bayram*.

V
"YOU BOUGHT A HOUSE *WHERE?*

A friendly sea,
This little Marmara unfurling at my door...
    James Lovett, "The Cordial,"
        in *Lovett's Turkish Album: Istanbul 1954-1995*

"So, is it like one of those Greek islands? Lots of old ladies in black and not much greenery? Do you ride donkeys or do they use camels there?"

"I hear you bought a whole island! Do you have to grow all your own food? Do you have electricity?"

These were some of the more ridiculous reactions as we began to tell friends in the United States about our house on Heybeliada. Some were horrified. They were the same ones who had cried "Professional suicide!" when we went to Turkey the first time, so we just ignored them. It is true, though, that nearly everyone has trouble picturing this little island so close to central Istanbul.

For that matter, many people have trouble picturing Turkey. The most common reaction is a polite comment like, "Wow, that sounds exotic!" Well, it is and it isn't.

Heybeliada, like Turkey, has two identities. Western Turkey is mostly modern, urban, and "European." The eastern part is far more traditional, rural, and "Middle Eastern." The population movements —village to city, east to west—in recent decades have blurred those traditional geographical divisions. On Heybeliada, we see both identities. Many islanders would blend easily into any small Anatolian village; others would be unremarkable in a Parisian café. This is a population that bridges East and West as clearly as Istanbul's two suspension spans across the Bosphorus. The "Western" and urban side of life feels familiar and comfortable. The more "Eastern" side adds piquancy. Like our Seattle friend with the *mas* in Provence, we wouldn't be happy with a purely rural or small-town life, but the island's village atmosphere and traditions are charming as part of the total Istanbul experience.

Heybeliada ("heh-beh-lee-ah-dah") is a mouthful for non-Turkish speakers, but its meaning is simple: "Saddlebag Island." When seen from afar, the two highest hills, separated by a green valley, are thought to resemble a saddlebag. The lower of the two hills, Ümit ("Hope") or more commonly Papaz ("Priest") Hill, is the site of the Greek Orthodox seminary; the higher one, Değirmen ("Windmill") Hill, is crowned by pine forest obscuring the vestiges of a long-ruined windmill, formerly used to grind the wheat and barley that once grew on Heybeliada. Our house, like most of the others, is on the eastern slopes of Değirmen Hill.

Second largest of the Princes' Islands, Heybeliada (or just "Heybeli") is only four kilometers from the Asian shore and covers 2.35 square kilometers, about three-fourths of which is protected pine forest. It's a nice size. If there were no city nearby, it would be far too small, but as a haven close to Istanbul, it is just right. The 5,500 year-round population swells to 30,000 in the summer months.

For someone seeking urban amenities, Heybeliada has plenty to offer. In the small shopping district near the ferry dock we can find everything from grocery stores to pharmacies, from ATMs to teahouses, from antiques shops to Internet cafés. In this small and friendly place, we can suggest new items to accommodating grocers, who are willing to stock brown rice or espresso or other non-traditional foods in hopes that we won't be the only ones interested in buying them.

Heybeliada has a good selection of restaurants, ranging from simple snack stands to more serious *meze* (Turkey's wonderful mixed hors d'oeuvres) and fish restaurants, some with live music on the weekends. Amusements include beaches, picnic grounds, walking trails, and, in summer, an outdoor cinema. There are small museums in the houses of Heybeli's two most famous former residents: Ismet Inönü, the Turkish Republic's first Prime Minister and second President, and prolific journalist and novelist Hüseyin Rahmi Gürpınar. If no one else is around, the caretaker at the Hüseyin Rahmi house will sometimes encourage a visitor to try on the great writer's hats.

Visitors to Istanbul, if they travel to the islands at all, usually go to the largest one, Büyükada, earlier known as Prinkipo, or the Prince's Island, in memory of Byzantine emperor Justin II's 6th century palace (no longer extant) on that island. The name "Princes' Islands" has come to be used for the archipelago as a whole, but the official name is just *Adalar*, the Islands.

The islands can be seen from the city. Some of the best views are from the hotel roof terraces in Sultanahmet, the area near the Blue Mosque. From there, you can recognize the islands by the communications towers atop Kınalı, the island closest to central Istanbul. On a clear day, the islands stand out; on hazy days they may be only vaguely visible. But they abide. And they have witnessed some intriguing bits of history. The Byzantine period was filled with conspiracy, murder, and mutilation (eye-gouging was a favorite way of discouraging rival princes), but later years brought less bloodthirsty highlights to the islands. Some of my favorite island factoids:

• Turkey's founding father, Mustafa Kemal Atatürk, an aficionado of the national drink, had his first glass of *rakı* here;

• Leon Trotsky's exile included five years' residence on Büyükada (1929-1933), where he wrote his *History of the Russian Revolution*;

• Sir Henry Bulwer, Ambassador of Great Britain to the Sublime Porte and brother of the novelist Bulwer-Lytton (of "it was a dark and stormy night" and "the pen is mightier than the sword" fame), built a castle on Yassı, one of the smaller islands, to remind him of his ancestral estate at Knebsworth in Hertfordshire;

• The future Pope John XXIII, Angelo Giuseppe Roncalli, lived in the Vatican's Büyükada villa when he was papal nuncio in Istanbul, 1934-1944. A neighbor, whose window overlooked the Vatican villa's garden, has described seeing the nuncio "stalking through the flower beds, reciting his daily office in loud and eloquent Latin, while behind him followed a fat little friar playing the violin."

Four of the nine islands (Kınalı, Burgaz, Heybeliada, and Büyükada) can be visited easily by ferryboat. Each has its individual character and traditional ethnic makeup. Kınalı ("henna-colored," so named for its red soil) has been predominantly Armenian since the late 1820s—or even earlier if you count some of the Byzantine rulers of Armenian heritage. It is basically a residential community with few remains of historical or aesthetic interest.

The next island, Burgaz (a corruption of *burgo* or "tower," named for a structure no longer extant) was until recent years populated by Greek fishermen and flower gardeners. The island's most famous resident was the beloved writer Sait Faik Abasıyanık; the house he occupied from 1934 to 1954 is now a museum in his memory. The Greek Orthodox church still dominates the main square, but today the island is increasingly favored by Muslim Alevis, the second largest religious group in Turkey.

Heybeliada lies between Burgaz and Büyükada ("Big Island"), the largest in both size and population. Büyükada is the islands' administrative center and the favorite of Istanbul's elite, government officials, and the Jewish community (it is still possible to hear Sephardic Jews conversing in Ladino). Although the ferry ride from Heybeliada takes only ten minutes, we don't go to Büyükada very often. We find it too crowded, too much like being in the city. But for a visitor, it has the best tourism facilities and the most beautiful examples of island architecture.

Heybeliada is a modest place compared to its larger neighbor and its population is the most Turkish of the islands. Some of our U.S. friends assumed we must have found a community of expatriates on the island, but there are few foreigners or non-Muslims living here…only a couple dozen Greeks, a handful of Americans, a few Armenian families, a surprising number of Suriyani Christians, and enough Jews to provide a *minyan* for the small synagogue. Residents range from old *Istanbullu* families to recent arrivals from Turkey's economically depressed eastern towns and villages. The island's beauty, history, and serenity attract Turkish intellectuals, writers, and artists—a few of them year-round, more during the summer. Among the summer residents is Orhan Pamuk, Turkey's best-known contemporary novelist.

The permanent residents may be fishermen, shopkeepers, teachers, or horse-carriage (*fayton*) drivers. Some islanders commute to businesses in the city. The Navy's high school brings naval families, and the officers' club is a favorite of retired admirals. Although Heybeliada was formerly 90% *Rum* (Greek), some of the Turkish families go back a long way. One family boasts of six generations in the *fayton* business. Members of some of these longtime Heybeli families are easily identified by distinctive physical resemblances. I always notice members of an extended family I think of as the Sean Penn look-alikes; the resemblance, even among the women, is remarkable.

We are pretty easy to spot, too. There are few foreigners on this island, so we tend to stand out. Even when we see people we don't know, they seem to know who we are. Early in our island days, Ben went into the local barber shop for the first time, explained that he wanted his hair left a bit long in back, "like an orchestra conductor." When the barber finished, he swept the towel away with a flourish and announced, "OK, Maestro Benjamin!" When we get into a *fayton* with a driver we're sure we haven't seen before, we give him the address and always get the reply, "*Biliyorum*" ("I know").

As in the rest of Istanbul, one of the fascinating things about life on Heybeliada is the mix of people. There's nothing homogeneous about this city or this island. Turks come from dozens of ethnic groups, forming a society nearly as pluralistic as ours in the United States. Some Turks have the Central Asian features of the early nomads; others, with roots in the Balkans, are blond and blue-eyed. In the city, neighborhoods reflect economic and social levels, but on Heybeliada all are thrown together in close proximity. On our street, poor families live next door to millionaires, women in village garb and headscarves chat with women in shorts, heart surgeons exchange greetings with garbage collectors, and children with homemade toys play in the streets with kids taking an outdoor break from their computers and DVD players.

******

Each season, too, has its fascination and beauty. Spring and early summer are the time for roses, wild and hybrid, in all colors, but mostly shades of red or pink. In fall, vines are heavy with grapes, and in spring their leaves are perfect for stuffing with rice, pine nuts, and currants as *dolma*. Pine forest dominates the island. Although the trees were a later addition to the island (early drawings show only low scrub), pine has a long and honored association in the Eastern Mediterranean as the tree associated with Cybele, the Titan earth goddess, mother of Zeus. Bacchus, too, would feel at home on this island: figs and grapes are well suited for the climate and flourish here. The dozens of other fruit-tree varieties dotted around the island—plum, cherry, loquat, pear to name only a few—are the vestiges of orchards that used to supply much of Istanbul's fruit.

******

Traces of Istanbul's colorful history are visible on Heybeliada and provide us another source of endless interest. Since the ninth century, this island has preserved its special character as a place of refuge or exile or, since the mid-19th century, escape and pleasure. As we wander around the island, we find traces of the Byzantine past—monasteries, sacred springs, churches—as well as examples of Ottoman architecture both simple and grand, both ruined and restored. For most of Istanbul's Ottoman period (15th-20th centuries), the islands were left to themselves, but in the 19th century, Heybeliada begin to shape its modern character.

There was a Greek commercial college as early as 1831, but few visitors came from the city. The boat trip by caique—the long, narrow Ottoman skiff powered by a team of rowers—took several hours each way and there were few amenities on the island. In mid-century, however, three events changed the island's destiny: the Sultan allowed foreigners and non-Muslims to buy property, steamship service to the islands began, and the Greek Orthodox seminary opened.

Rum families began to build summer homes to enjoy Heybeliada, now within easy steamship reach. Our house, farther up the hill than the earliest villas, was built somewhat later, in 1904. Seminary and commercial school students' visiting families needed lodging, so grand and simple hotels were built to accommodate them. Today's five-star Halki Palas Hotel was originally built in the 1850s for those visitors. The first homes were simple wooden ones, but the trend was soon toward larger villas. The carpenters' guild, at its height, numbered more than sixty craftsmen, and Italian architects were brought in to propagate styles popular in Western Europe. That was the golden age of Heybeliada.

The most famous place on the island in its heyday was Çam Limanı bay, where *Istanbullu*s gathered on weekend evenings in *gazino*s (outdoor cafés) with soft light from lanterns. Music, mostly guitar, came from all sides. Couples or groups joined in the singing or rented small boats to row in the moonlight. Greeks and Turks drank together and sang together, and islanders still talk wistfully of those days, of the moonlight, of the indigo water, of the aromas of grilled fish and pine forest and sea foam, of the sounds of music and laughter that went into the wee hours.

Ibrahim was the first to tell us these stories of Heybeli's "good old days." But when we made the half-hour hike to Çam Limanı to get a whiff of the past, we found that the lanterns, the cafés, the graceful small boats are long gone. Only a makeshift lean-to remains, offering rental paddleboats, cold drinks, and simple snacks. The beach is mostly deserted except for the occasional fisherman repairing his nets or young boys having a swim. Across the road is a vacation facility for Health Ministry employees. It is cheap—its only apparent attraction—and it is close to the water, but the people staying there look bored and melancholy. Turkish arabesque music sometimes blares from a scratchy radio.

The only visitors to Çam Limanı now are the yachts—large and small, Turkish and foreign—that moor in the bay on summer nights.

But the yachtsmen seldom step onto the island, and no effort is made to offer attractive facilities to them. It is a missed opportunity, but the islands are gaining renewed popularity as a weekend escape for Istanbul families and as a vacation spot for Greeks, so there may be hope for restoring Çam Limanı's former beauty and gaiety.

Heybeli's Turkish residents miss the old days. They all tell us how much livelier and richer life was when the *Rumlar* were here. I can't remember ever hearing anti-Greek sentiment (except, perhaps, exasperation with Greek government policies) among our islanders. They seem to understand that although a sea, a language, and a religion divide them, they have a lot in common.

Longtime islanders may yearn for the bygone days, but the islands' greatest beauties are, we hope, immutable: the clean air, the sweet aroma of roses and jasmine, the tranquility, and the ever-changing colors and light. On a hazy morning, with just a few fishing boats clustered together at a promising spot, the Asian shore is barely visible, but as the sun breaks through the haze, it creates a dazzling sparkle around the boats. On mornings like this, the buildings on the other islands may be invisible, giving the impression of nothing but pine forest.

There are some—whether in Istanbul or on Heybeliada—who see only what *isn't* there, who regret the passing of the good old days. But the city and the island can still bewitch those willing to fall under the spell. For them and for us, *these* are the good old days. Discontent with present-day conditions seems to be an old island tradition. In 1862, about fifteen years after the introduction of steamboat travel to the islands, one observer wrote:

> Those who remember the islands, not 30 and 40 years ago, but only 15 years ago, will seek in vain today for the pleasing calm and solitude which they sought and found every year in the islands as they fled the noise and tumult of the city.

Another Heybeliada tradition is that you are not really an *adalı* (islander) until you have climbed the highest hill, Değirmen, and found the ruined windmill there. When you do, you also find wonderful sweeping views of the islands and the city. In the foreground is the lush green of Heybeli's forest and, in the near distance, a full view of Burgaz, Kınalı, and three smaller islands. In the far distance, the Istanbul skyline, with Haghia Sophia and the Blue Mosque, is clearly visible. Looking the other way, the expanding new suburbs of Asian Istanbul stretch as far as eye can see. Just below the crest of Değirmen Hill—far higher than the horse carriages can reach—are the simplest houses on the island. Here, at the end of a steep climb, where more affluent—or perhaps lazier— residents refuse to live, are ramshackle houses with million-dollar views.

For many years, the past was shoved aside to make way for modernization, but now Turks have come to terms with both and are building on past glories as well as present opportunities. When we first moved to the island, many of the older houses were in poor condition; some had been abandoned by their owners, and a few had squatters living in them. We used to pass by them, saying, "What a shame. If only someone would buy this one and fix it before it's too late." But today a revival of interest in things Ottoman is rescuing many of Heybeliada's lovely houses. Each year, a few more are restored to their original beauty. Each restoration is like a miraculous rebirth.

These buildings provide a context of past glory, while the energy and vitality of Turkish youth promise great things to come. With its sweeping view of Byzantine, Ottoman, and sprawling modern Istanbul, the top of Heybeliada is an ideal vantage point for dreaming of good times past and future.

VI
TAKING POSSESSION

Property is a piece of one's soul.
Turkish proverb

When Sevin completed the house deal for us—months after we had first started the process—we were already in Brussels at our new jobs. Ben was happily arranging cultural events and exchange programs between Belgium and the United States; I was discovering that working with the European Union is unbearably tedious unless you are a lawyer or a policy wonk. I am neither of those, so it seemed an eternity until spring when I could return to the island for a few weeks. Now that the house was ours, we could take the next steps toward "getting" there. The spring visit would start the process. It would be a long time before we could finally start "being" there.

On a Saturday in mid-April, I left the rain and chill of Brussels for the bright sunshine of Istanbul. April can be unpredictable in Istanbul, with the possibility of anything from warm days to rain to, occasionally, snow. This was my first April on the island, my first time there as owner of the house, and *kısmet* made it one of Istanbul's loveliest Aprils in a decade.

Going directly from the airport to the Sirkeci ferry dock, I found that I had about forty-five minutes until the next boat to the islands. After the flight, I was glad to have time to relax in the sunshine and enjoy the view across the Golden Horn, noticing that the Galata Tower had gotten a new "witch's cap" while we were away.

The quiet reverie was broken when an old woman, Nuray Hanım, sat next to me and started asking questions. When she learned I was on my way to Heybeliada, she informed me that she is a year-round Heybeli resident, married to a retired lawyer. Taking advantage of someone new to hear her stories and complaints, she began a monologue that lasted the entire trip: "The island isn't what it used to be…too many new buildings…greenery disappearing…no longer safe…all the fault of those people moving here from the east…What? You're here by yourself? Hope you have good locks; don't open the door to anyone at night…" and on and on.

When we arrived at Heybeli, I had my first lesson in island economics. Nuray Hanım talked to the *hamal* (porter), instructing him to take our bags to the *fayton* stop where we could get a horse carriage. When I offered the *hamal* a small tip, the amount recommended by Nuray, he stared at it with disbelief and sneered, "What is this? Soup money?" He was expecting something five times higher. I soon learned to ignore the advice of island retirees who seem unaware of changing prices. The porters are indulgent with old-timers living on inadequate pensions. A new arrival, however, is in a different category.

Before getting into a *fayton,* I realized that I would not be able to stay in the house—no bed, no kitchen equipment, and who knows what condition after the winter. A new, inexpensive pension had opened just across from the *fayton* stop, so I left my luggage there and told them I'd be staying for a few days. Although the walk up to the house takes only a few minutes, it seemed right to make this first trip by *fayton*. It was a good choice.

The *fayton* takes a longer route, the direct way being too steep for the horses. We followed the island's main road toward the forest, passing along the principal residential street, past some of the grandest of the island's mansions. Making a U-turn just in front of the Navy's preparatory school at the edge of the forest, the driver switched back onto the upper, parallel road and urged the horses into a gallop to make it up the grade. Once on the upper road, I could admire some of the island's loveliest gardens and sea views.

The *fayton* dropped me at the door of our Heybeliada house…the first time I would enter it as owner. It was just as exciting to me as it had been at first glance, but the garden was even more overgrown after several more months of neglect. A wooden bench near the front fence was broken and rotting. It was impossible to see the path, but I carefully moved leaves and branches aside to make my way to the front door of the house, unlocked the door, and stepped in.

The winter hadn't been too hard on the house. There was surprisingly little dust, a few dead bees. No sign of rats or mice or major problems, except for a bit of water damage from a hole in the roof over one room. There were a few pieces of furniture, including a faded but usable Art Deco-style sofa and chairs. This was a little bonus extracted by Sevin after we had left for Brussels. As part of the final contract, Sevin had insisted that Bingül leave some of the furniture for our use. At least I had a place to sit. Relieved to be in our house at last, I tried out the Art Deco chair, opened the bottle of wine I'd brought for the occasion, poured a glass, and walked slowly through each room, savoring the beautiful and pondering the unacceptable.

The walls were covered with floral wallpaper, peeling in some places, and dominated by the unsightly fuse box I remembered from the first visit. The floors were overlaid with linoleum discolored by years of wear. When we eventually removed it, we found beautiful, thick wooden planks that had been protected by the ugly covering. The room partition, with its makeshift plywood "panes" instead of glass, was as unsightly as I remembered it. My first thought was to tear the partition out, making the central room larger. But that kind of decision would have to wait until we had advice from an architect or contractor.

The best room at this point was the living room with its balcony facing the sea. The sofa and chairs were in need of new upholstery, but their wooden frames were solid. They would do for a start. The walls in this room continued the floral wallpaper motif, but there was lovely detail that could be uncovered and highlighted. The French doors to the covered balcony opened easily, and the balcony itself seemed solid. On each side of the French doors, the now bare windows revealed their generous size and elegant pattern of panes.

The other room on this side of the house had been used as a heavily draped bedroom, but was now empty of any furnishings. The handsome proportions in both rooms became apparent, and the large windows, facing east toward the Sea of Marmara and Asia, were poised to let in the morning light. Our living room would be the room with the balcony, but what to do with this other room facing the sea? That decision could wait, but this room needed immediate attention. The water damage in one corner, from a leak somewhere in the roof, would have to be fixed before the next rains.

The bedroom on the opposite side of the hall had peeling paint on the ceiling and the now familiar flowered wallpaper. One panel drooped down, and I couldn't resist the temptation to tear it off as a first step toward erasing Bingül's traces from the house. There were solid wood shutters on the bedroom window facing the terrace. They remain to this day—just right for providing privacy while letting in a bit of air and light.

So far, so good. The bones were even better than they had seemed when I first saw the house. The makeup didn't seem impossible to fix.

Behind the house was the terrace where Bingül had served tea and cake that first day. After a brief sunny space just outside the house, the terrace was surrounded by grapevines, rose bushes, and a wall of hydrangea intertwined with the upper branches of a large bay tree planted in the garden below. The old grapevines had trunks the size of small trees, and the grape arbor, supported by metal poles, was a crisscross of rotting wood laths, mostly broken. The grapevines were piled deep above them, blocking most of the sun directly above. The hydrangea and bay branches nearly touched the trailing vines and effectively obliterated the sea view. The effect was more cave than garden.

******

By now it was late afternoon. I had no phone at this early stage, so I walked to Ibrahim's house to let him know I'd arrived and to see if he had some suggestions for the roof. His apartment is on the ground floor of a large and gracious old building on Refah Şehitleri Caddesi, the main avenue stretching from the shopping area to the edge of the forest, the same road I had traveled a few hours earlier by *fayton*.

Behind his building, an orchard and forest area slopes sharply down to the island's principal beach. Ibrahim's apartment is the most modest of the five in the building and may have been the service area originally. Its large patio and surrounding greenery compensate for the low ceilings and dark rooms. Ibrahim is not a man to throw money away. Each year he decides on one single project to improve his apartment…new tiles for the patio or a sunroom off the living room or better kitchen cabinets. *Adım adım,* step by step, is his watchword. He proudly showed me his project for the upcoming season: an outdoor bar as pictured in the Turkish version of *Maison Française* magazine.

Ibrahim said the roof problem was easy. Mehmet Ali was the island's roof man. The island's *only* roof man. Ibrahim explained, "The islands used to have lots of very good *usta*s, skilled workmen. Many were Greek, some Turkish. The Greeks left years ago, and many of the best Turkish craftsmen and skilled workers have gone to Germany where they can earn more money. The ones still here are good, but sometimes not as good as the ones who left. We're lucky. Mehmet Ali is the only roofer left on Heybeliada, but he does good work." He phoned Mehmet Ali, who agreed to come to the house on Monday morning to inspect the roof—unless rain prevented him.

As we sat in Ibrahim's small garden, overlooking the first bit of forest at the edge of Heybeli's settled area, I began to forget all my doubts and anxieties and remembered why we'd bought a house on this island. The evening was calm and cool; the air was filled with pine aroma and the sound of seagulls and crows. The evening breeze from the northeast rustled the leaves and, since it was not yet high season, there were few signs of human activity other than the occasional horse carriage driving by or mothers calling their children to come in for dinner. I told Ibrahim about Nuray Hanım on the ferry. "Nonsense," he said. "These old women have nothing to do but complain. The island is wonderful and the safest place on earth."

We turned to the bigger question: who could help us with fixing up the house? I reminded Ibrahim that we didn't have a lot of money to do this work. We wanted the house to be solid and secure, but couldn't throw money around too lavishly. He understood perfectly.

"My good friends Sadi and Beyhan," he said, "have a daughter, Günhan, who is an architect. She helps me with my projects. Maybe she can help you."

As he described Günhan, though, she sounded too inexperienced. She had a master's degree in restoration from Istanbul's leading architecture department, but so far had never actually done any major restoration work. Architecture is a very competitive profession in Turkey and most young graduates work for large firms to get established. Beyhan and Sadi's daughter wanted to remain independent and, so far, had gotten mostly interior decoration jobs. This didn't sound too promising. I said as much to Ibrahim, but he was sure she'd be fine. Even so, I thought we'd better look for other options. At this stage, we had no idea how much work might be involved, so we had to be sure the person we hired would be qualified for anything we might need.

American friends are often surprised that the lawyer and the architect recommended to us were women, but Turkish women have had equal access to the professions longer than their American sisters. This, like so many other facts of Turkish life, requires a word about the national reverence for Mustafa Kemal Atatürk. Any visitor to Turkey is immediately aware of the omnipresence of statues, paintings, murals, and photos of the founder of the Turkish republic. Though he died in 1938, Atatürk remains very much a part of daily life. His reforms in the 1920s and 1930s were so bold and so broad that there is hardly a single facet of modern Turkish life that isn't linked in some way to his legacy. As he built a new nation almost out of thin air after the devastations of World War I and its aftermath, he changed everything from the legal structure to the alphabet, from women's status to men's hats.

One of his boldest reforms was to provide the legal framework for women's equality in the new republic. Turkish women's suffrage came in 1930, just two years after British women won equal voting rights and twenty-two years before Greek women enjoyed the same privilege. In the villages, women's legal rights improved much more slowly and are still hotly debated in today's Turkey. So-called "honor" killings remain an unfortunate reality in many rural areas, and domestic abuse is far too common throughout the country.

For decades, however, entry into prestigious Turkish university departments of medicine, law, architecture, and other professions has been based on ranking in the university entrance exam, where girls often outperform the boys. Women are well represented in the professions, and Turkey has had a female prime minister. In the cities, there is nothing unusual about women lawyers, architects, doctors, university presidents, or CEOs. Turkey's largest holding companies are family-owned enterprises, and when the patriarch of one of them died in 2004, the company came under the direction of his niece, the founder's choice over his male relatives. Sevin and Günhan are part of Atatürk's legacy, too.

******

Ibrahim and I talked a bit more about the house. Now that I had seen it again, I was impatient to stay there. With his help, I was able to find basic furnishings at a shop on the main street and arrange for delivery the next morning. I would have to stay only one night at the hotel.

Ibrahim insisted on showing me around on Sunday after the delivery. It came on time, and by mid-day we were exploring the island, meeting some of the shopkeepers, and having lunch at the naval officers' club, where I met some of Ibrahim's former colleagues. In the late afternoon, we sat on Ibrahim's patio, where I met his upstairs neighbor, Zeyyat, a writer whose short stories describe island life.

A gentle, soft-spoken man then in his 70s, Zeyyat loved to sit on his wide porch facing the main street where he could observe island life going by. His stories capture the essence of Heybeliada, particularly as it was a generation ago. Zeyyat turned out to be a film buff as well, and we spent the first of many afternoons comparing movie notes and quoting lines to each other while drinking endless cups of the strong coffee he favored. When we tired of movies, he always had more stories to tell about island life and history. When my Turkish faltered, he tried to help by explaining in German, his only foreign language, never remembering that I can't understand a word of German.

That first evening we all went to Ibrahim's favorite fish restaurant on the seaside, where the *rakı* flowed freely, the food was delicious, and recorded music added to the cheerful atmosphere. It was a chance, too, to get a look at our fellow islanders.

Since it was the weekend, the restaurant was full. The mild weather encouraged nearly everyone to sit at the outside tables, to the delight of the ever-present stray cats, always looking for handouts. There were several families, and though the hour was getting late, their very youngest children were there, too, digging into the *meze* selections and chasing the cats. There were some couples quietly dining together at the smaller side tables, well out of the way of a large group of men all trying to outdo each other in the *rakı* department. I was especially struck by a handsome group of young people, probably students, in their jeans, t-shirts, and other universal garb. They seemed indistinguishable from similar groups anywhere in Europe or the United States, though most of the girls were impossibly slim and chic. Some of the customers live on the island, but this small restaurant, Ibrahim explained, has become a favorite with young people who live on the Asian side of Istanbul. It's a short ferry ride from Bostancı to Heybeliada for an inexpensive seaside meal and a break from the hectic pace of the upscale shops and restaurants on Bağdat Caddesi, the broad avenue stretching along the Asian shore.

There wasn't a headscarf to be seen at the restaurant, though the influx of villagers to the city has made this traditional head-covering a more common urban sight that it was, say, a generation ago. The island, like other parts of Istanbul, has a mix of modern and traditional, of Western and Eastern, of rich and poor, of tank tops and headscarves. Though we see some of these more conservative families in the teashops or picnicking in the forest, they seldom turn up in these seaside fish restaurants. Theirs is often a transplanted village life that retains the old customs and only gradually becomes urbanized. Many of these families, for example, still use a *görücü* (matchmaker) to find husbands for their daughters, and some words and phrases that were strange to me turned out to be village usage. This is not the place for a discussion of transplanted village life in Turkish cities, but the often-uneasy transition has sparked some of Turkey's most contentious debates. The place of the headscarf, an unacceptable religious symbol for many in this secular nation, is as controversial in Istanbul as it is in Paris. But the island tends to ignore many of the issues that rear their head in town, preferring to maintain its traditional distance from urban concerns.

*****

The next morning, the sun was shining, so Mehmet Ali and his two assistants arrived to inspect the roof. As Mehmet Ali began to climb onto the roof, two seagulls, protecting a nest, flew at him with shrieks. He wasn't surprised or fazed by this.

"They're on all the rooftops," he explained. "Can't avoid them in this season."

Staying clear of the nest, he and his workers approached the other side of the roof, where the work needed to be done. Once they had cleared away the winter's debris, they found the problem immediately—not one hole, but three.

Mehmet Ali, well into his fifties and a good forty pounds overweight, clambered around on the roof, shouting orders to his semi-skilled assistants. From time to time, he would call information down to me, most of which I didn't understand, but each time it was followed by *"Başka çare yok!"* ("That's the only solution!") The whole job was done within three hours and the total charge was the lira equivalent of $35. When the roof work was finished, I offered them tea, one of the few things I could do in my semi-camping state. I should have known better. That's not the way Turkish hospitality works.

"No," Mehmet Ali immediately said. "You are the newcomer. You must come to my house, meet my wife, and have tea with us. She's expecting you. It's on the next street down the hill."

His young assistant noticed that I had no heating in the house.

Heading out the door, he asked me to wait before going with Mehmet Ali. Within five minutes, he was back, struggling to carry a large heater powered by a heavy gas cylinder. "Here," he said, "You'll need this for these chilly April nights. You can give it back next month when it gets warmer." I was deeply touched. This young worker, who lives just up the street, had brought the heater from his home, presumably depriving his own family of at least one room's heat, maybe their only heat, in order to show kindness to a foreigner and a new neighbor.

Mehmet Ali's home turned out to be a small, ground-floor apartment in a two-story concrete building. Simply furnished but spotlessly clean, the apartment was filled with family photos, a large television, and a small table set for three. Mehmet Ali's wife—dressed in a villager's traditional modest long skirt, headscarf, and layers of sweaters—had prepared "snacks" to rival high tea in a London club. She filled my plate with homemade cake, salty biscuits, assorted cookies, a spicy bulgur salad called *kısır,* and cheese-filled *börek* pastries. As we washed all of this down with strong Turkish tea, she told me about their son in Germany, proudly showing photos of the grandchildren she sees only once a year, when they come to the island for their brief vacation. The food was enough to feed at least a dozen, rather than three, but Turkish hospitality demands a lavish spread. The surroundings may be simple, but the hospitality is always regal.

VII
THE ISLAND WAY

Qui a bon voisin a bon matin.
                    French proverb

Now the die was cast. We owned the house and planned to make a life on this island. But what did we know about it, really? We had enough experience in Turkey to know that we would be treated well, but how would we begin to meet people and find new friends? Would we find kindred souls? Would the islanders be open to foreigners in their midst?

Ben came from Brussels several days later, and Ibrahim began to arrange for us to meet people he thought we should know.

I had noticed and admired a beautiful house nearby—a large wooden villa with an onion-dome tower. Ibrahim promised to introduce us to the owners: a businessman who has spent summers on the island all his life and his American wife, a fine classical pianist. Ibrahim must have mentioned us to them soon after our conversation; they turned up the next evening at the front gate. A tall, slim, and elegant couple then in their 50s, Judy and Tunç warmly welcomed us to the island and said they were on their way to have drinks with Ayla, who lives on our block. It was a good chance, they said, to begin meeting our new neighbors. Others turned up, too. There was Cengiz, a longtime islander, and another Turkish-American couple, Atilla and Lynn. I wondered if the island would turn out to be full of Americans, but, in fact, Judy and Lynn are the only others I've met. Atilla is an avid sportsman who keeps up a rigorous regime of running, rowing, and sailing. Lynn, who wisely stays far away from that much exercise, is a diva with the Istanbul Opera. Not long after meeting them, someone in the city said she knew an opera singer on our island, "a lovely blonde American woman with a beautiful smile." There couldn't be two American opera singers here, could there? But Lynn had dark brown hair.

Puzzled, I asked Lynn, who laughed and explained, "I'll soon be doing *Carmen,* so I have to be brunette for the next few weeks."

All of us crowded into Ayla's small apartment for drinks that evening, our first experience of something our friend Kadri calls "the island way." In the city, Turks would never think of just dropping in, but they revel in the informal atmosphere on the island. The "island way" accepts, even encourages, drop-ins and impromptu gatherings. For newcomers like Ben and me, this was a wonderful way to meet people. This was, in fact, how we first met Kadri, a cheerful and talkative businessman turned university professor.

One day, we went to look for Ibrahim, but when he wasn't there, ended up sipping coffee on Zeyyat's front porch, just a few feet from Ibrahim's apartment. We were on our third or fourth strong coffee and had concluded friendly arguments about which Hitchcock movie was really the best. Zeyyat stubbornly insisted on *Psycho,* but finally confessed it was because one of the island houses reminds him of the Bates Motel. Always ready to answer our questions about island history and lore, Zeyyat agreed to teach us the famous song about summer evenings at Çam Limanı bay during Heybeliada's golden age. As we were attempting to stay in tune with our enthusiastic rendition of *"Biz Heybeli'de her gece..."* ("On Heybeli we went out every night lost in joy and delight in our rowboats in the moonlight..."), Kadri happened to pass by, heard the voices from Zeyyat's porch, and came to investigate.

Once Kadri arrived, Zeyyat said very little, ceding the floor to Kadri, who began expounding his theory of the "island way." To put his theory into immediate practice, Kadri insisted that we come right then—unannounced—to his house where we could meet his wife, Nilgün, on one of the rare days when her job with the Istanbul arts foundation didn't keep her in the city until very late. I didn't know it then, but when we returned to live in Istanbul the next year, Nilgün would be one of the people I worked with most closely as I managed the consulate's cultural affairs.

But our first encounter with "the island way" was that evening at

Ayla's apartment. Everyone was having a good time. There had been no plans to have dinner together, but no one wanted to end the evening. Tunç and Judy, who have the largest house, suggested we pool whatever we had in our refrigerators, bring things to their house, and have dinner in their garden. We had little to offer, not even a refrigerator, but could contribute a bottle of French wine I'd brought from Brussels. It turned out to be a welcome novelty. The Turkish wine industry has been well protected from competition, and foreign wines are hard to find.

We shared dishes of cold green beans in olive oil, fried eggplant and peppers with yogurt, a salad of white beans (*piyaz*), followed by a mixed grill cooked over a quickly prepared barbecue, a rice pilaf with pine nuts and currants, and some of the fresh artichokes abundant at the farmers market that week. Dessert was, as it usually is on the island, a selection of the season's best fruit. This was just an impromptu potluck dinner, but could not have been better if it had been long planned. Our bottle of French wine was followed by plenty of the local red.

As the evening wore on, Cengiz chided Tunç for speaking English to us—"How are they going to improve their Turkish if you speak English to them?"—then insisted on telling stories in English, or occasionally French, infuriating Ayla, who understands only Turkish. Some of the stories, pieces of Ottoman history, were about his grandfather, a guardian of the Prophet Mohammed's tomb in Medina, who had rescued some of the relics from the English and delivered them to the Sultan in Istanbul. Some stories were slightly wacky: "My family origins are in Georgia, where Adam, the first man, came from." Others were island stories, travel stories, jokes.

I tried my best to keep up, head spinning, in the jumble of languages. But all in all, I got the comfortable feeling that these people, with decidedly unfamiliar family histories and names like Atilla and Cengiz (the Turkish form of Genghis), were not so different from friends back home. Despite our diverse backgrounds, we had very similar ways of looking at the world. By the end of the evening, it was clear that Ben and I were going to be happy here.

Well past midnight, we all said goodnight, kissing each other on both cheeks as Turkish friends always do.

In the years since that first dinner, the warm, informal "island way" has been another reason for feeling at home on Heybeliada. This island, far from our American roots, can feel as laid back and friendly as San Francisco. In some countries, foreigners find it difficult or uninviting to penetrate the local society. Expatriates in those places find themselves isolated, having little real contact with the "locals." In some countries, expatriates even find themselves in separate compounds. Not so in Turkey. Especially not so in Istanbul. It has been a cosmopolitan city for centuries, with a rich mix of nationalities, cultures, and religions, and with a tradition of acceptance and openness.

On Heybeliada, the same holds true. We didn't know the island in the days when it was predominantly Greek, but today's Turkish population has made us feel at home from the beginning. We are known as foreigners, of course, but this seems to have become less a curiosity and more a convenient way to describe us, like saying someone has red hair or uses a cane. At first, we were given the special hospitality reserved for foreign visitors, but now we are mostly considered part of the scene, just another *adalı* (islander) couple, albeit different from the others.

Even casual visitors to Turkey notice and appreciate the extraordinary, justly famous hospitality toward foreigners. The Turkish word for it is *misafirperverlik,* and it seems to be deeply ingrained. Perhaps this goes back to the early Turkic nomads who knew that anyone who turned up at their tent must be in need of rest and refreshment. Some say it is the legacy of the *hans,* the inns spaced a day's travel apart along the Silk Road. Or maybe it is just a kind of civility that has died in the West and survived in Turkey. Whatever the reason, a Turk will never let a visitor enter his home or office without offering at least a glass of tea.

It is nearly impossible for a foreigner in Turkey to pick up the check when dining with a Turk. I know. I've been trying for years to treat my friend Jale to a good dinner. When we are in Ankara, where she lives, she invokes *misafirperverlik*. "This is my town," she says, "I'm host." I've tried everything. Once I got up mid-meal, saying I was going to the ladies' room, but actually sneaking over to the cashier to give him my credit card. Jale wasn't fooled. In fact, she had left *her* credit card with him when she arrived. When she came to Istanbul, I thought this would be my chance. After all, I'm the one who lives in Istanbul; this Ankara resident would be the guest in my city. She would have nothing to do with this idea. "I am the Turk," she said. "You are the foreigner. I am host." We met in the city and, when the waiter at the small Bosphorus-side restaurant brought the bill, she explained to him that this foreigner was trying to pay when she, the Turk, must do so. Anything else would be *ayıp* (shameful). The waiter, of course, agreed. My only hope is to get Jale to the island. I know I can count on the waiters at the Halki Restaurant, where we frequently bring our visitors. Once in a while, a guest may slip inside to pay the bill before we have the chance. Inevitably, the guest is brought back to the table like a naughty child. The waiters would never let us, as island residents, bear the shame of letting a visitor pay for the meal.

Though we also patronize many of the other restaurants on Heybeliada, my fondness for the Halki Restaurant goes back to those first days on the island. When Sevin came to the island to deliver the deed and other papers, we decided to celebrate with a nice fish lunch. With nothing but an electric teapot in the house, eating out was the only choice. As we walked along the seafront, looking at each restaurant, trying to choose, something drew us to the smallest of them: Halki, the Greek name for Heybeliada. It looked simple and unpretentious, and the customers looked happy.

It was another bit of *kısmet*. After that first meal with Sevin, I came under the protection of Erdinç, then the Halki's cook. At first I assumed this was his restaurant, but soon learned that the Halki is owned by Kazim Bey and his sons, a longtime island family. They became part of our lives on the island in later years, but during those first days, I knew only Erdinç, a small, slender man with a cigarette permanently fixed to the side of his mouth, and a slightly harried look around the eyes. His raspy voice showed the effect of years of those cigarettes. He looked to be in his late 40s or early 50s.

The food was good at Halki, so I kept going back. Ben hadn't arrived yet, but Erdinç took good care of the island's new foreigner. He wouldn't trust the waiter to get everything right, left the kitchen to take my order himself, and, if the restaurant wasn't too crowded, often stopped to sit and chat.

Turkish restaurants treat their "regulars" well, offering coffee or tea or a dessert fruit plate on the house. They also pride themselves on remembering what you like. After I had once asked for a *sade* (no sugar) Turkish coffee, Erdinç simply produced one at the end of each meal. Soon he was also wordlessly presenting mint liqueur in a small glass coated with powdered sugar—gift of the house. The taste was cloying, but I felt obliged to drink it. I don't really like Turkish coffee, and have one only rarely. And I could certainly do without the sweet liqueur. I thought I'd better try to break this automatic chain of Turkish coffees with a Nescafe, the only other option in traditional Turkish restaurants.

"Do you have any Nescafe on hand?" I asked Erdinç.

"Of course, of course. Right away," he replied. With his next breath, he called over to the restaurant next door: "Do you have any Nescafe over there?"

Most days Erdinç paid little attention to how he was dressed, but on Saturday and Sunday, he was in his finest for the weekend tourist crowd: white pants, white tie, colorful shirt, freshly starched chef's hat. It's Saturday night, I thought one evening, why not some wine with dinner? I asked Erdinç for a half-bottle of Yakut, then the most popular Turkish red wine…"if you have some on hand." It was the Nescafe routine all over again. "Of course, of course." Turning to the young apprentice, Erdinç whispered to him, stuffed some money in his hand, and sent him off. Some time later, the boy returned with a half bottle of a rival brand I had tried elsewhere and didn't much like. I said nothing. Erdinç praised the wine, opened it with a flourish, and assured me that this was much better than Yakut. By now understanding that there were no other half bottles of wine on the island, I thanked him for this new "discovery" and finished my dinner. That evening, my coffee was accompanied by rose liqueur instead of mint, but it was equally unpalatable. Erdinç joined me, constantly smoking, as I tried to finish the last of my food and coffee through the haze of smoke.

The next year, when Ben and I had a proper kitchen in our house, we seldom ate out. One day, Erdinç stopped us on the street to ask with some concern, "Where are you eating these days?" The Halki became our usual restaurant, the one to which we often took friends and visitors. We began calling it the *küçük* (little) Halki, to distinguish it from the Halki Palas, a five-star establishment in a renovated building near Ibrahim's house.

The *küçük* Halki has now become one of the most popular restaurants on Heybeliada, but Erdinç is long gone. His health began to fail, and the cigarettes didn't help. He left his job as Halki cook, briefly worked elsewhere, but finally set up a stand selling homemade pickles. Whenever he saw us, he called to us, suggested having a tea somewhere, and hoped we'd buy some of his pickles. He tried to keep up appearances, but his health continued to decline, and when we returned to the island one spring after a few months in California, he was nowhere to be seen. He had died that winter.

We are still loyal to the *küçük* Halki. Kazım Bey and his sons have upscaled the restaurant with better décor, a full range of wines, well-trained waiters, and a cook whose creations are more sophisticated than Erdinç's traditional dishes. It's a different place now. A better restaurant, if truth be told. But whenever I am there, Erdinç comes back to mind. I miss him, though maybe not his sugared mint liqueur.

VIII
BOO RADLEY ON THE BOSPHORUS

It isn't easy being a Turk.
    Turkish saying

OK, some might say, so Heybeli is a nice island, Istanbul is an interesting city, but why Turkey? Isn't it awfully dangerous there? Won't you have to wear a veil and give up driving a car? Aren't the fundamentalists taking over? Don't they hate Americans?

When I hear these kinds of questions, I hardly know where to begin. Turkey is probably the world's least understood place. It is the Boo Radley of countries. Just as young Scout in *To Kill A Mockingbird* was terrified of her mysterious neighbor, Boo Radley, many Westerners are afraid of Turkey. Like Scout, though, they may find that once they take the time to listen and understand, the fearsome will turn out to be something quite different from what they expected. Yes, Turkey has its faults. Can you name a place that doesn't? But much of what people think they "know" about Turkey is dead wrong.

To understand why a foreigner would want to live on Heybeliada, you need to get beyond clichés about Turkey and Turks. Try a word association test with the word "Turk." A European's response might be "hopeless EU candidate" whereas the American's only association may be *Midnight Express*. On either continent, the answer is too often unflattering to the Turks.

Let me digress for a moment.

It is not surprising that Turkey's efforts to join the European Union have encountered so much resistance. European history has been filled with tales of "the terrible Turk" since 1071, when the fierce Seljuk Turks, led by Alp Arslan, decisively defeated the Byzantines in the battle of Manzikert in eastern Turkey, near Lake Van. In Europe, the Turk became a symbol of barbarism and cruelty, both to the defeated Byzantines and to the Crusaders, who responded to Pope Urban II's call to reclaim the Holy Land. The first crusade began only twenty-five years after the Battle of Manzikert.

By 1453, when the Ottoman sultan Mehmet II conquered Constantinople, the once grand Byzantine capital was a shadow of its former glory and fell easily to the Turks. Constantinople became Istanbul, the Ottomans' political and religious center. At its height, the Ottoman Empire extended across much of North Africa, most of the Middle East, and well into southeastern Europe. The empire was strong and the possibility of its conquering more of Europe was not to be dismissed lightly. For centuries—through the Renaissance, through the Enlightenment, through the Industrial Revolution—the Ottomans remained the "other," the infidel, not part of Europe but intricately woven into Europe's destiny. As the Ottoman Empire declined in the late 19th and early 20th century, it became known as "the sick man of Europe." Note: *of Europe*.

Even today a lot of emotional baggage remains from the centuries of fearing that the Turks might breach the walls of Vienna or beyond. When I visited Budapest with Sevin not so long ago, hatred of the Turk was still palpable, though the Ottoman conquest of Buda was in 1541. I think I was even more outraged than Sevin at the way she was treated at passport control and at the hotel. Today, after more than eighty years of the secular, western-oriented Turkish republic, many Europeans continue to think of it only as Muslim, threatening, and exotic.

Americans, on the other hand, tend to have few ideas about Turkey. Ben and I certainly fell into that category; we knew next to nothing about Turkey before coming here the first time. American tourism to Turkey is growing, but the numbers are still far lower than those for France or Italy or Greece. Many Americans aren't even sure where Turkey is. Once when I was speaking to an American student group, one of the girls proudly told me she knew about Istanbul: "the only city on two continents..." (so far, so good) "...Europe and Africa" (oops).

If pressed to search their minds for a context for Turkey, movie-minded Americans might come up with *Topkapı*, Jules Dassin's delightful adaptation of Eric Ambler's *Light of Day*. Unfortunately, the more common connection is with *Midnight Express*, the 1978 Alan Parker film scripted by Oliver Stone. It's unfortunate that after more than twenty-five years, that film is still many Americans' only context for Turkey even though the author of *Midnight Express* complained about the movie's distortion of his book.

But, for the most part, Turkey doesn't have a lot of visibility in the United States, though there are some who think they "know" that it is on the brink of becoming "another Iran." This is not the place for an analysis of Turkish politics, but suffice to say that what may appear to the West to be a rise of Islamic fundamentalism in Turkey is more accurately described in socio-economic terms. As conservative villagers moved into the cities, the entrenched and often corrupt power elite ignored or vilified them. Meanwhile, other parties with conservative and/or religious tendencies reached out to these poorer voters. They not only help them, but also share many of the same conservative "family values." It is a 21st century example of old Chicago-style politics: if one party ignores you and the other provides you with support and social services, which one are you going to vote for? If one party has become a symbol of corruption and another preaches a return to traditional values, which one is going to appeal to conservative voters?

The November 2002 electoral victory of the Justice and Development Party (AKP or AK party in Turkish), whose leaders cut their political teeth in Islamist parties, owed more to voter disgust with the rampant corruption in the more secular parties than to a desire for Islamic rule. Some of the secular elite saw only a threat to Atatürk's secular, Western vision, but the new government—the first stable, non-coalition government in years—has made striking progress toward needed democratic reforms and closer links to the European Union. Some see this as the equivalent of Nixon's overtures to China: sometimes the least likely source can bring about the needed change.

Some foreigners find themselves unable to reconcile the many sides of this hard-to-pigeonhole nation—always the bridge between East and West, strongly tied to both worlds, but not fully part of either. How, they wonder, can Turkey pull off the hat trick of being one of the strongest members of NATO, holding the leadership of the Organization of the Islamic Conference, and maintaining its close relationship with Israel—all at the same time? Turkey was the third country (after the U.S. and USSR) and the first Muslim nation to recognize the state of Israel. And the Turkish-U.S. strategic relationship has been a crucial one for more than fifty years. Unfortunately, these alliances are not without cost to Turkey. Their support for the U.S.-led 1991 Gulf War meant tens of billions of dollars in lost trade and revenue. In November 2003, when Istanbul suffered carefully orchestrated bombings of synagogues and British-owned targets, it became a new battleground in the continuing international war against terrorism.

Why do Americans know so little about Turkey? One reason is lack of experience with Turkish-Americans, who are not one of the most visible ethnic groups. There are only a few hundred thousand Turkish-Americans, mostly well-educated professionals who assimilate easily and quickly into the mainstream. Although there is a network of Turkish-American associations, there is little effort toward developing a Turkish lobby like the powerful Greek- or Armenian-American ones. Turks are not comfortable with self-promotion. That is one of their charming qualities—a rare modesty—but it also makes for very poor public relations efforts.

An American diplomat in Turkey once said in exasperation, "No Turk yet has been born with a PR gene." There may be something to that. The common image of the Turk is so far removed from the Turks I've known that it may be due to an utter lack of public relations savvy, an incapacity to project the right image.

A couple of classic examples: After the first Gulf War in 1991, Turkish tourism was a disaster. Cancellations flowed in. The Ministry of Tourism needed a campaign to convince foreign visitors that Turkey was a safe place to holiday. Their solution: large posters showing a yacht moored in a seductive azure lagoon, but with the slogan: "Come see our war ships." Not the kind of irony likely to convince the wary traveler.

In 2003, after the Iraq War, cancellations once again showered down on Turkish tourism. By May, when the tourist traffic began to revive a bit, I received an e-mail from a Turkish travel agent. Subject line: "Explosion expected at Turkish tourist resorts." Hmm, I wondered, what threat have they heard about? The message was, in fact, offering rock-bottom rates, "exploding" the usual prices. Cute, but guaranteed to remind the nervous tourist that Iraq doesn't look so far away from Turkey's beaches.

We have invited many American friends to visit us on Heybeliada and have arranged itineraries for them to travel elsewhere in Turkey. Some are reluctant to come but are finally convinced to give it a try. We have found that Americans' lack of knowledge about Turkey becomes an advantage. They carry none of the negative historical baggage that Europeans seem reluctant to shed. It is a rare American who dislikes Turkey after spending some time here. Not just "Oh, yeah, it was fine. Good food, interesting history." No, they become besotted with the place. One friend from New York even became convinced that she was a Turk in a previous life.

There does seem to be a natural affinity between Turks and Americans. More often than not, they feel comfortable with each other and genuinely like each other…and, at least in the case of Americans, are often surprised by that. Since the start of the Iraq War, there has been a lot of talk about anti-Americanism in Turkey, but much of that is anti-Bush Administration, not anti-American, sentiment. On a person-to-person level, Turks and Americans continue to get along just fine.

What brings an American to Turkey? There is no significant number of American students studying in Turkey, even though many Turkish universities teach entirely in English. American business investment in Turkey is growing, but slowly. Europeans often come to Turkey seeking sun and beaches, but Americans can find those closer to home and need other reasons. For one-time visitors, it is often no more than a "been there, done that" tourist destination. Something to check off the list of world places to visit.

But what about those who return or stay long enough to dig into the place? Some come for the history and splendid monuments. One expatriate Istanbul acquaintance of ours has little interest in contemporary Turkey, spending all his time and attention on Byzantine remains. Foreign archeologists have endless possibilities in a land that has seen dozens of civilizations and cultures come and go. Istanbul has been home to three empires of different faiths. It's heaven for a history buff.

Others are charmed by Turkish traditions, attending every folk dance performance and craft fair they can find, but many of these never look beyond the local color. Not that there is anything wrong with local color. One of my fondest Turkish memories is watching a line of young men on the shore of Lake Van, moving joyfully, in perfect unison, in an impromptu rendition of the local folk dance, set against the backdrop of the vast blue expanse.

Some foreign visitors, in "foodie" searches for new flavors and ingredients, delve into the complex mix of traditions that make up Turkish cuisine. One of the best introductions to this delectable part of Turkey is in the late Alan Davidson's wonderful *Oxford Companion to Food*; he rightly states that Turkey is "a country whose history is mirrored in its food."

The rapidly changing Turkish political and economic scene intrigues some residents, such as diplomatic personnel or business executives, but others never take much interest in the country at all. An unusually honest diplomat, when I asked him about his thoughts at the end of his three-year tour of duty in Turkey, replied, "I haven't spent any time in Turkey; I've only been in the diplomatic community."

Some, especially young teachers, want an adventure, a chance to experience something new and different. For them, Turkey's relatively low cost of living has been an added incentive. That was what brought Ben and me to Turkey the first time.

We were looking for overseas teaching jobs and found them in

Ankara, but our ignorance of Turkey and its past was abysmal. As we discovered more about the country, we became increasingly fascinated by it. This was a treasure trove of history and literature. The landmass that is today's Turkey was the birthplace of Abraham, King Midas, Homer, Aesop, Herodotous, St. Paul, and even the original Santa Claus: St. Nicholas. This is where Noah's ark landed, where Julius Caesar said, "Veni, vidi, vici," where Alexander the Great cut the Gordion Knot, where the Trojan War took place, where the Amazons lived, where Holland's tulips came from, where Marc Antony met Cleopatra. Good grief. Why didn't we know any of this? Turkey, it turns out, is the world's best-kept secret.

But many places have a rich history, natural beauties, colorful folkways, and varied cuisine. What makes Turkey so special? What accounts for the strong pull it turned out to have on us?

There's a simple answer: the Turks themselves. Nearly any foreigner who has settled in Turkey will say the same thing. The rich mix in Turkey makes for a fascinating and pleasing blend of contradictory traits: pride and modesty, emotion and reticence, Mediterranean and Asian. It is always dangerous to generalize, but certain characteristics seem to stand out as typically Turkish. Although I have met a rude or obnoxious Turk from time to time, it is a rare event. Most often I find a grace and dignity all too scarce in many other cultures. The old-fashioned civility and gentility are natural and refreshing, not at all stuffy or insincere. The Turks themselves show little patience with the occasional exception to this, such as the *maganda*, a type of macho lout found in urban areas. Another exception would be the aggressive touts who hover around tourist centers.

Turks have a reputation as dour, laconic people, but the strong Mediterranean side to their character contradicts the stereotype. After an initial reticence (that grace and dignity), Turks reveal their Mediterranean warmth. Hugs or kisses are the normal greeting between friends, men or women, and Turks show no self-consciousness in telling friends they love them or stating matter-of-factly, "Ahmet dropped by yesterday. He loves me very much."

Though a charming trait, it was as startling to me as the first time I heard a Frenchman refer to himself as an intellectual, something an American would consider presumptuous and pompous.

Our first time in Turkey was an education and a revelation. We vowed to come back if we could, and finally managed to do so years later. It was no longer the same Turkey we'd known twenty years earlier, but it was even more appealing. We soon knew that we wouldn't leave again.

The new Turkey still has the history, beauty, cuisine, and wonderful people, but now boasts a stimulating artistic and intellectual scene as well as one of the most dynamic young populations in the world. It is a country on the move and even *Newsweek* magazine in 2005 declared "cool" Istanbul to be "the best place in the world to be young."

Why would Americans or other foreigners want to live in Turkey? Maybe a better question is: Why wouldn't they?

IX
BRINGING UP THE HOUSE

I want a house that has got over all its troubles; I don't want to spend the rest of my life bringing up a young and inexperienced house.
                Jerome K. Jerome, *They and I*

It is a long way from a vague feeling that you'd like to live somewhere to the reality of being there and feeling settled. Even buying the house was only the first step. When I returned to Heybeliada that first April after we bought the house, our plans were still vague. We had jobs in Brussels. This was just a brief visit. When could we expect to move back to Istanbul? Would we ever be able to use the house as more than a summer place? Were our friends and family right this time? Had our whim led us into something more than we could handle?

Ben joined me for part of the visit, but we didn't have much time to work with an architect or contractor. The house seemed solid and in need of only some TLC and cosmetic improvement. But we needed some professional advice in order to be sure and to help us decide how to proceed.

We felt uncertain about the experience and qualifications of the young architect Ibrahim had suggested and thought we'd better look for other options. Alper, who had solved our insurance problem and advised us on banks, had an architect to recommend: the one who had built his house, one of the island's nicer modern buildings. Built on an odd bit of land, the house is brilliantly designed to use the space wisely and seize every opportunity for a view or a shaded garden. The architect responsible for this, Yakup, has an office in one of the poshest business districts of Istanbul. That should have been my clue, but having no other options yet, I called Yakup to arrange a meeting.

Yakup and his associate, Faruk, came to the island one afternoon to see the house and discuss our needs. We went over the whole building. While they found it to be fairly solid, they said there would be major work to do.

"Most of the wood is rotten," Yakup said, "and before any remodeling can be done, you'll need to do insulation against the island humidity and a fair number of structural repairs. I know these old houses. I've worked on dozens of them. You can't go at it piecemeal. It needs thorough, careful work and you have to work from the bottom up. Make sure the foundation is good, and build up from there. All this will take time, of course."

Yakup pointed out some original features that should be kept and recommended removing others that were later, inauthentic additions. He would need a little time to work out some specific recommendations and estimates, but saw this as a long process, probably eight months to a year. During this April/May visit, we would have time only for essential repairs and development of The

Plan, he explained. Nothing could be done during the high season when noisy construction work is forbidden on these tranquil islands. Only in fall or winter could the actual work begin.

My heart sank even deeper than it had over the insurance glitch. What kind of bottom line could Yakup be thinking about? We agreed to meet again in two weeks. That would give them time to pull together an initial proposal. I sent Yakup and Faruk off to the ferry and began to think over what they'd said. We seemed to have gotten ourselves into something more than we'd expected.

Trying to look on the bright side, I thought, well, maybe this is better. We can spend this first visit just thinking about what we want to do. Yes, then we can turn it over to the experts, walking away from the chaos. We might need to return to Turkey from Brussels at some point to check on the progress, but the next summer everything would be perfect. Beautifully refinished floors would be ready for our carpets, new paint would bring out the beauty of the rooms, better appliances and fixtures would add to the comfort, and we'd just concentrate on a few final touches.

These were the ravings of a madwoman. The scenario was impossibly optimistic, but these were early times.

While I was indulging in this fantasy, Mehmet Ali came by to check on the roof. We'd had some rain since his repair work, so he wanted to be sure no problems had developed. I mentioned the architect's visit.

"Yakup Bey?" he repeated. "I don't trust him. There's something about his eyes."

Of course, I should have guessed that he would know Yakup. Everyone who lives or works on the island seems to know everyone else.

"Believe me, he'll try to get as much money as he can out of you. I was working across the street when your house was painted last year. There's nothing wrong with the wood—except for one part of the balcony. I can show you where. That you'll have to fix. *Başka çare yok.*" (Once again his favorite phrase: "no other solution.") "But that's all. You'd be crazy to replace the rest. The wood is good."

I mentioned Ibrahim's young architect.

"That's what you should do. *Başka çare yok*," said Mehmet Ali, with conviction. "She's just right."

"Do you know her?" I asked.

"No, but I know Ibrahim. You should trust his judgment. *Çok efendi bir adam.*" This, we've learned, is roughly the equivalent of calling someone a class act.

I wanted to agree with Mehmet Ali and Ibrahim, but neither is an architect. Maybe the place really did need substantial remodeling. And maybe Yakup's price wouldn't be so bad. He certainly had the experience that Ibrahim's young friend lacked. There would be no point hiring someone cheaper, then having it all redone by Yakup.

When the day of our appointment with Yakup arrived, we took the ferry into Istanbul and a taxi to Yakup's office in an ultra-modern high-rise building in one of the newly developed business areas. Most of Istanbul—and nearly everywhere on the islands—remains at human scale. There is plenty of land west and east of the city, so development mostly spreads out rather than up. But a few districts have been zoned as commercial centers where developers can satisfy their pent-up need to build skyscrapers. Yakup's office is in one of those.

Yakup and Faruk were prepared with extensive suggestions and plans. We were still puzzled, though, that they seemed to want to tear down most of the existing structure and rebuild from the ground up. We didn't want a new house; that's why we bought the one we did. Wasn't there another, less drastic option?

"I know these old houses," Yakup reminded us. "You can patch them up to a point, but they won't last. You need to do a thorough job at the beginning. Then it will last forever."

This was far more extreme than what we had in mind, but he's the architect and should know about these things. He had some plans we could take home to study. As the meeting ended, we approached the delicate subject.

"What kind of money are we talking about here?" we asked.

"Everything included. Best materials and workmen. Our careful attention to every detail...let's see, total for everything, even the garden..." He punched a few numbers into the calculator on his desk, looked up, and quoted a number well over twice what we had paid for the house.

Ben and I looked at each other, unable to speak. In shock, we were finally able to end the meeting with a feeble "We'll look over the plans and let you know." We left the building, half hoping the elevator would crash to the ground and kill us.

Now what? First we had to use *torpil* (influence) to insure the place, now we seemed to be facing restoration costs well beyond our means. We returned to the island in a deep depression, looking at the house with different eyes, wondering why we'd blown a major part of our savings on a white elephant.

Ibrahim dropped by that evening for a *rakı* and listened to the story of our day with Yakup.

"*Tabii,* of course," he said, "Alper is a millionaire, you know. His architect is one of the best and most expensive in the city. You don't need that. You can do a little now, a little later. *Adım adım.*"

Ibrahim's advice was clear.

"These houses were built with extra-wide planks of Romanian pine." Ibrahim was especially proud of this point since his family came from Romania, part of the Ottoman Empire at the time this house was built. "Look at your house compared with some of the modern ones. These were built to last. You don't need a complete renovation. Just some improvements. Yakup Bey is not what you need. He works with rich people. You should hire Beyhan and Sadi's daughter, Günhan."

What other choice do we have, we thought. We need to find a solution. Let's talk to her.

******

Two days later, Günhan arrived at the house with Ibrahim, who had gone to the ferry dock to meet her. In her late 20s, with large, dark eyes and a short, gamin haircut, standing only about 5'2", Günhan looked more schoolgirl than architect. She was a bit shy about her English, but our Turkish vocabulary didn't include much in the way of architectural terms at that point. We took Günhan around the house. She looked carefully at each room, her eyes growing larger and brighter at every step.

"This is a wonderful house," she said, "I hope you will like for me to work here."

We sat outside with tea and snacks and talked with her about her background and her initial thoughts. She said the first step would be to check for rotten wood or faulty insulation. She and the expensive architects agreed on that, but we still weren't entirely convinced. Despite her academic degrees, the fact of her inexperience remained. It was not yet clear how much work we would really need to do on the house. We wondered whether she'd be up to the demands. We also wondered how a slip of a girl like Günhan would fare with workmen and craftsmen, the *usta*s. Would someone like Mehmet Ali take orders from a Günhan?

After Günhan left to catch her boat back to Istanbul, we sat with Ibrahim to talk it through. We mentioned all our misgivings. He tried to smooth over them.

"She is a clever girl," he said. As we got to know Ibrahim better, we learned that this is one of his highest compliments. "She knows what to do, and, if she finds a problem she can't solve, she will consult with her more experienced professional friends. She wants this job very much and will do her very best for you."

He paused briefly, then added, "Also, she will not charge you very much. I told her so."

We thought about it for another day. We weren't entirely convinced about Günhan, but we certainly couldn't work with Yakup. We could begin looking for other options, but time was short. There was, finally, one convincing factor. One architect wanted to tear down the house and start over. The other's eyes sparkled as she looked at each detail of the house. Yes, Günhan appreciated the house, just as we did. She would treat it with respect and bring it back to life. If she turned out to be a bad choice, so be it. Was this another of those "irrational" decisions that turn out to have been exactly right? Absolutely. It was *kısmet*.

X
THE *USTA* QUEEN

Everything is easy in an *usta*'s hands.
—Turkish proverb

Hiring Günhan may have been one of the smartest things we ever did—probably smarter than buying the house in the first place. Once she finished up a small job or two, she was ready to work with us.

"Günhan" is an unusual name in Turkey—"day" (*gün*) plus "sovereign" (*han*—the Turkish form of *khan*, as in Genghis or Kubla). We teased her that her name must mean "Queen for a Day." Having no knowledge of the old daytime TV show, she was puzzled by the joke, but took it in stride. What she also took in stride was the need to dominate the workmen and craftsmen—the *usta*s—she would contract with to do our work. Maybe not Queen for a Day, but she proved to be a fine Usta Queen.

As Ibrahim had warned us, many of the younger *usta*s have gone to Germany, where they can earn much more. Some of the older *usta*s are ready to retire and don't really have the strength to do much work anymore. A fine *usta* at a good price is becoming hard to find. Günhan, we learned, has a knack for finding them. Once we saw her in action with our first *usta*, we put aside any doubts about Günhan's ability to handle them. Turkey is a hierarchical country and there was no doubt about who was the boss. She had the qualifications and the title, so she had earned the right to supervise them. She always treats the *usta*s with respect, but expects them in return to respect her standards of quality and timing. In most cases, she was able to negotiate the lowest possible prices. The exceptions were those who didn't really want the job and quoted an impossible price to avoid saying No.

But the *usta*s began to appear a bit later. First we had to think through what we wanted to do with the house. Never having done anything remotely like this before, we had no idea where to start.

There seemed to be a lot of basic infrastructure decisions to be made. The fun part seemed a long way off.

"Insulation," Günhan insisted, "is the first priority." Winters on the island produce a damp environment with inevitable humidity leading to mold. She continued: "Then someone will need to look at the exterior wood." We wondered who was right. Mehmet Ali or Yakup? How much rotten wood would we find? We began to see that there would be several options, but none had to be as extreme as what Yakup had proposed. His proposals were the gold standard and probably would have been wonderful, but they were well out of our league.

Günhan was our main consultant and had excellent ideas, but each person we talked with added to our understanding. One evening, as Ben and I sat outside, we heard someone at the front gate. Before he was even inside the garden, he was calling to us in English:

"Hello. Anybody here? I'm Bülent, your neighbor over there," he said pointing across the street and down the block. "Do you have a cold beer?"

Before we could reply, Bülent, who already knew that Americans had moved in, was shaking our hands and asking our names, where we were from, why we were here, and a thousand other questions. When we had the chance to ask questions, we learned that he is an engineer, a graduate of Istanbul's French-medium schools and a longtime Heybeliada summer resident. Our conversations end up being a Babel of English, French, and Turkish, and his comments are usually punctuated by his ever-present FDR-style cigarette holder. Whatever language he is using, his conversation is always lively and full of island lore. At our first meeting in the garden, he kept peering toward the inside of the house. We took the hint and asked if he'd like to look around.

As someone with good knowledge of the island, Bülent was able to answer our questions about the original floor plan. The partition upstairs (the one with plywood where colored glass should be) was, he confirmed, original—it was to divide the stairwell from the central room. Downstairs, he showed us how the original entrance to the house led to double doors that would have opened to a stairway. It made perfect sense. This was a good lesson in taking our time— *adım adım*—before making decisions.

******

During this visit to the island, though, we had little time. We had to be back in Brussels by June 1, and we were already well into May. This was no vacation. We had to set up bank accounts, transfer electricity and water accounts to our names, get a phone line, buy a few household items, and, mostly, consult with Günhan. We needed to make a lot of decisions quickly, work out a plan, and decide how much to do and on what schedule.

We considered bringing the house back to its original configuration, but modern lifestyles make the old room arrangements less convenient. No one these days wants the kitchen in the basement and the dining room upstairs. It soon became clear that the whole process would be much simpler if we could avoid breaking into walls or making any other major changes. The downstairs was already a separate apartment and could remain that way as guest quarters. As it turned out, the house did not need any structural alterations, and we were relieved to find that Mehmet Ali had been right about the wood. It was solid. There was no need for major repair or replacement. We would be able to get by mostly with just sprucing up the interior.

As we had noted when we first saw the house, the bones were good. But to protect those bones, Günhan insisted on checking the insulation. This was the unglamorous, but crucial first step. It was also her first chance to prove she was up to the job.

She called in two insulation specialists to get their evaluation. Since many of the wooden houses on the islands are closed up during the winter months, they suffer from moisture and buildup of *küf* (mold and mildew). The insulation experts pointed out that the worst *küf* was in the rooms next to the *sarnıç,* the rainwater cistern downstairs. They warned that it is impossible to avoid mildew in those rooms. Like termites in the Florida keys, island *küf* cannot be eradicated, only slowed down. "Why not get rid of the cistern?" they asked. But we wondered about water shortages. A cistern can collect rainwater all winter to provide for summer garden needs.

There is little natural water on the islands. There are a few wells and, here and there, traces of an old Greek *ayazma* (sacred spring), but these could never supply the thousands of residents today. Where did the water come from, then? We soon learned that a large tanker docked daily at the fishing marina, bringing the island's water supply from the mainland. The water was pumped through a large pipe to a reservoir on top of the highest hill, from which it was distributed, using force of gravity, back down to the houses. Although this seemed to work well, a new system began a couple of years later. New underwater pipes, leading from the mainland, now ensure constant water supply without relying on tankers.

Despite the *küf* problem, we wanted to keep the *sarnıç* as a part of the house's Ottoman past. The cistern—ten by ten feet and about six feet deep—has access only through a hatch in the back hallway. The *usta*s would have to empty whatever water was there, get down into the cistern, clean it thoroughly, install the insulation, and reopen it. I shuddered to think what might be down there, but they went to work cheerfully and checked for vulnerable spots in the rooms next to the cistern. The test would be the level of *küf* the next spring.

In the first years it seemed that blistered paint and *küf* were inevitable. The problem dominated island conversations the way wine varietals might in the Napa Valley. While visiting neighbors one evening, we were invited to see their newly *küf*-free guest room on the lower floor. What was their secret? They had put in a false second wall, making the room a bit smaller, but presumably trapping the *küf* out of sight. It seemed to me that this was something of an *"Après moi, le déluge"* approach—wouldn't someone, someday have to deal with what was behind the wall? Probably, they admitted, but maybe not in their lifetime.

Our *sarnıç* stayed, but so did the *küf*. Finally, the solution appeared as Ben and I traveled up Barbaros Boulevard in Istanbul one day. A huge banner: *"Hoşça kal, küf!"* ("So long, mildew!")

stretched across the front of a shop. We went in to investigate. A dehumidifier from the U.K. was on display. The salesman gave a good pitch, and there was a guarantee. The price was high, but lower than the likely cost of repainting every year. We tried it. It works. *Hoşça kal, küf!*

But that was much later. That first spring we had more than just *küf* to think about. We began to work out plans with Günhan so that she could deal with the house while we were back in Brussels. Ben and I were new to this kind of thing, and I soon learned that I do not have the nerves or stomach for it. I can't really visualize the final product (I always performed miserably on spatial concept tests in school), and quickly become bored by things like faucets and curtain rods. Günhan figured this out even before I did and led me along *adım adım*, carefully protecting me from the worst of it.

Luckily, most of the work was done while Ben and I were in Brussels. Once Günhan had a good idea of what we wanted, she could carry on in our absence. While we were gone, there was perfect symbiosis: she sent progress reports to us, and we sent money to her.

As the plans progressed, we decided that the living room should have a *sedir,* Turkey's traditional long, low, deep divan. Wooden bookcases could be built into the niches in another room, and a wardrobe was needed in the bedroom. For all of these, Günhan contracted with Ali, one of the last of the old-line carpenters. He was an old man—this was one of the last jobs he would do—and showed the effect of years of hard work, even a missing first finger on his left hand. But he also had a level of skill and professionalism that is too often lacking in the younger *usta*s.

He was also one of the few *usta*s who came ready to work. The average *usta* takes a casual, Allah-will-provide approach to job preparedness. Most of them bring no ladder, no sawhorse, not even the most basic tools. We saw one *usta* using a paring knife to saw a piece of wood; another found a piece of broken glass to clean off some varnish. One was planning to saw planks on top of our dining room table until we stopped him…not quite in time. When another *usta* arrived to install some colored glass, he brought only a small bag with a glass cutter and putty. As he began work, I couldn't watch. He stood on the front windowsill, holding on to the house, and reached up to install the glass. He had no ladder, no safety net, nothing to stop him from falling to the concrete, fence spikes, or rose thorns below. He could not understand what I was worried about.

And yet, their work always turned out just fine. Likewise, the key maker on the island has an operation that does not immediately instill confidence. Cemal is, as far as we know, the only *anahtarcı* (key maker) on the island. He also sells lighters, key chains, and other odds and ends. He has no shop, just an open-air stand next to the newspaper kiosk on the way to the ferry landing. If he's there, it's service while you wait. Or he can come to you if it's urgent. He now has a cell phone, but when we first met him he simply gave customers the number of the public telephone booth next to the kiosk. If he heard it ring, he answered it. Nothing at his stand said so, but on the island, you are just supposed to know or to ask around. There, as elsewhere on the island, things are pretty informal and low-tech. Since he has no shop, Cemal has no electrical outlet, but he runs a line to the newspaper kiosk to do the basic work. Then he switches to a measuring stick and hand file to finish the keys. Cemal's work is slow but sure...and every key he has ever made for us has worked perfectly.

When we returned to Brussels, the island's summer season—and its ban on construction noise—was about to begin. Little could be done until the fall. Before we left, though, Günhan insisted that we meet and talk with each *usta,* partly because personal contact makes such a difference in Turkey, and partly to be sure everyone understood the plans the same way. It was also time for specifics: *which* refrigerator, *which* sink, *which* door handles, *which* curtain rods? In Kadıköy, on the Asian side of Istanbul, there is a neighborhood devoted to electrical, plumbing, and other household needs. Günhan lives nearby, knows the dealers, and can get good discounts from them.

We started looking. I hated every minute of it. Not much of a shopper in any case, I would easily prefer a root canal to looking at hardware stores and contractors' supply shops. Some of Günhan's clients have infinite patience with this kind of shopping, know exactly what they want, and can become very difficult if the perfect drawer pull isn't found. But Ben and I had no strong preconceptions, only vague ideas of what we might like, or what we definitely didn't want. When presented with dozens of choices, my mind froze, so Günhan did pre-visits to the shops, setting aside two or three choices that seemed to fill the bill. I could deal with that limited selection. As I look back, I realize that Günhan's quiet efforts made this a pretty minor task for us.

Even so, I had the impression that my life was nothing but a parade of bath fixtures and kitchen appliances. This was not entirely inaccurate. When we visited a friend's new apartment in a village up the Bosphorus, I slipped away to use the powder room and was appalled to find that I immediately knew the brand and model name of their newly installed toilet.

In June we returned to Brussels, as scheduled, with full confidence in Günhan's professionalism. And we were prepared to leave many details to her own good taste. She had unfailing instincts about where we would have specific demands and where she could use her creativity to freelance a bit.

When we returned the next summer, there was more work to be finished, so we did not entirely escape the *usta*s. Over the winter, the carpenter had repaired the pergola on the upper terrace, providing just the right spot to sit—under the grape vines, next to the fragrant jasmine and honeysuckle, and looking out at the Sea of Marmara. The grape vines stretched beyond the pergola toward the main house, but were supported only by some unreliable poles. Ben decided to have the carpenter build a second pergola to provide better support for them. Although I thought it was an excellent idea, I groaned at the thought of more *usta* time. When would we finally have our quiet retreat?

A week or so later, I went to Ankara to visit a friend and was gone only overnight. When I returned, the new pergola was there! Ben explained, "I told Günhan the *usta* had to do the job in one day. Otherwise, if you came home and found him working, you would kill me, then her, then the *usta*." He was probably right.

XI
CAPABILITY BEN

It's th' best fun I ever had in my life—shut in here an' wakenin' up a garden.
Frances Hodgson Burnett, *The Secret Garden*

At the end of that summer, I sighed as we packed to return to Brussels. I missed the excitement of Istanbul and the warmth of the Turks when living in gray, cold Brussels among the gray, cold Belgians.

As we were settling back into our life of *moules, frites* and rain, *kısmet* intervened again. There was a job opening at the U.S. consulate in Istanbul and it was just the one I qualified for: director of education, culture and media programs. With perfect synchronization, Ben had just completed enough years to retire from the foreign service. It meant leaving Brussels ahead of schedule, but there would be no lack of eager souls anxious to transfer there. Briefly: I got the job, Brussels agreed to release us, and Ben was hired to teach at a private university in Istanbul. So the Cassandras were wrong again. Our whim could now become our home.

When we moved back to Istanbul, we could do the finishing touches on the house. We began to look for furniture, lamps, window shades, and other pieces that would suit the Ottoman look. Colored glass replaced the plywood in the main hall's partition, as well as the top panes of the living room windows, creating pleasing refractions and changing colors throughout the day. The sheer white curtains in the same room billow in and out of the French doors as the breeze carries them. For lamps, we went to the Hor Hor antiques market in old Istanbul, where one shop specializes in reproductions of Ottoman lighting. There were beautiful Ottoman- or Victorian-style ceiling lights and others resembling the slim, oval lamps in mosques.

This was certainly more fun than sinks and toilets. And it allowed us to become better acquainted with the island's own antiques dealer, Naci, who claims to sell only items from houses on the island. He has successfully tempted us with everything from glass jars to tables, and we still drop by at least once or twice a week to see what's new.

Ibrahim arrived one day with a horse cart and driver, who proceeded to bring in a dining table and six chairs. Ibrahim never revealed where he had gotten them, but insisted there was no cost. They were in pretty bad shape, but once cleaned up and given new cushions, they were fine. *Adım adım,* the house began to fill up and look like a real home.

Meanwhile, the garden needed some attention. Up to now, we had made only half-hearted efforts, but now we were back to stay and could begin to deal with it. When we were away, we both had a vague memory of thick, unruly growth, but no specific recollection of what was there. Now we looked more carefully and saw the ruins of a once lush garden.

It was romantic, yes, but on the melancholy side. Everywhere we looked, there were vines, trees, and plants twisted together, with the heads of tea roses poking through the jungle of shrubbery, suggesting more sophisticated planting lurking below. The path to the house was just barely visible through the jumble.

There are natural-born gardeners. I am married to one. And there are those for whom there is no worse drudgery than spending a day in the hot sun and dirt. I am one of those. I appreciate the results of the work and am happy to reward the gardener with a glass of white wine, but I have no desire to participate.

The garden was, therefore, left to Ben, who saw himself as a latter-day Lancelot "Capability" Brown, the 18th century British landscape architect who showed clients the garden "capabilities" of their untamed property. But this, of course, was not a British garden. Ben wanted this to be a proper Turkish or Ottoman garden, but what should that be? A seventeenth-century Venetian in Istanbul, Ottaviano Bon, gave one of the best and most succinct descriptions: "A few shady trees, a view, a rosebud, and the sound of a nightingale will transform any garden into a Turkish garden."

Throughout the Ottoman Empire, and on into the Turkish republic, gardens and flowers were always an essential part of life. There has been a long tradition of gardens in many Islamic civilizations—the Koran imagines paradise as a beautiful garden filled with trees and flowers and running water. Earthly gardens are meant to be both a hint of heaven and a reflection of order on earth. But Ottoman gardens didn't entirely fit the Islamic garden tradition. As in so many other ways, Turkey was a bridge between cultures and traditions, in this case linking southern European and southwest Asian flora. Other influences, as Nurhan Atasoy explains in her extensively researched *A Garden for the Sultan* (the source of most of this background information), included the rich variety of Anatolian soils and climates, the influence of Byzantine predecessors (and their extensive use of cypress trees), European practices introduced by 19th century foreign gardeners brought to Istanbul, and the opportunities and limitations of the land to be developed into a garden. There are no examples today of a purely "Ottoman" garden, but historical accounts give an idea of how they must have looked.

Evidence of the Turkish love of gardens and flowers is easy to find. In Turkish, a place of peace and harmony is described as being "like a rose garden" (*güllük gülistanlık*). Despite the Ottomans' reputation as fierce warriors ready to conquer all of Europe, a famous portrait of Sultan Mehmet the Conqueror shows him holding a single flower. Many place names in Istanbul are related to gardens: Dolmabahçe ("filled garden"), Bostancı ("market gardener"), Yeşilköy ("green village"), Bahçeşehir ("garden city"), to name only a few. European history's most remarkable floral influence from Turkey was, of course, the tulip. First introduced into Western

Europe in the 16th century, the tulip became the most sought-after flower, reaching the level of "tulipomania" by the 17th century, when enormous prices were demanded for the best varieties.

The finest Ottoman gardens were, as one might expect, connected to the palaces, but the common man soon began to cultivate more modest examples. In today's overcrowded Istanbul, dominated by apartment buildings, a private garden has become almost as rare a luxury as one of those 17th century tulips. This is another advantage of life on the Princes' Islands. It is one of the few parts of the city where a house and garden can still be affordable. But until the most recent decades' huge population influx, the average *Istanbullu*s were able to enjoy their own gardens, which often included vegetables as well as flowers and fruit trees. The descriptions of these earlier gardens sound very much like our Heybeliada garden. Or at least as it must have been in its more cared-for days. Now it was in sore need of an Istanbul-based Capability Brown.

Capability Ben decided he would need some help and began to ask around for available gardeners. Several turned up to inquire about the job, but, after one look at the state of the garden, each suddenly remembered another pressing job that wouldn't end for a month or so. For the next few weeks, Ben plunged into it alone.

Each morning he put on a heavy shirt, strong jeans, and the thickest garden gloves he could find. Armed with large clippers and a machete, he did a fine imitation of Humphrey Bogart in *The African Queen,* wading and slashing through the vines, returning inside only when he had once again been torn up by thorns and needed something to stop the bleeding.

Behind the overgrowth and undergrowth, an earlier, thoughtful planting began to emerge. We created an image in our minds of a former owner, perhaps in the 1940s or 1950s, who created a garden both beautiful and practical. A 1934 photograph in Nejat Gülen's *Heybeliada* shows a school outing in what was then an open meadow. Our house, in the background of the scene, has no garden…only a line of laundry and a single tree.

Our imagined owner, following the Ottoman tradition, believed that a garden should offer beautiful aromas, varied colors, and an edible harvest. The trees in the garden, in varying states of health, included an enormous bay, a very productive loquat, a wild plum, a fan palm, two oleanders, and a scraggly pine looking unlikely to survive. The abundant grapevines on the property turned out to be *çavuş,* a large sweet white grape much prized by Heybeliada residents, both for its delicious fruit and for its tender leaves. We have a steady stream of neighbors asking permission to pick the leaves to stuff with rice and spices as *dolma.*

Given our experience with this garden, I would not object to hopeless endangerment or even extinction for the trumpet plant, an aggressive climbing plant that seems to grow before our eyes. It covered everything and attracted what seemed like every bee on the island. Though I like the image of Yeats' peaceful "bee-loud glade" in his *Lake Isle of Innisfree,* there can be too much of a good thing.

As Ben hacked away the old, unwanted growth, he uncovered pink tea roses, red climbing roses, white rambling roses, calla lilies, honeysuckle, and a host of other plants that had somehow hibernated and survived despite being deprived of sun for who knows how long. He was pleased to find that our Greek house had an abundance of acanthus plants, as stylized on Corinthian columns, and he was astonished to unveil a second wild plum tree that had been completely obscured by the hated trumpet plant.

After the worst of the trumpet had been removed, we heard odd sounds during the night coming from a corner of the garden, just below the bay tree. Investigating with a flashlight, we found a hedgehog, whose cover had been disturbed. He remained with us for a few more days—neighbors say a resident hedgehog is considered *kısmetli* (lucky)—but finally moved on when he saw there was no place left to hide.

At the end of each day, Ben was energized by the progress made, but full of wounds from his war with the weeds. Aching muscles, scraped joints, and rapidly eroding gloves were taking some of the fun out of the venture. Our neighbor Kadri provided a solution. He had long employed an island resident, Halil, to help with his gardening and do some of the heavy work. A few days later Halil reported for work.

Halil is short and wiry with a loud voice and nearly incomprehensible accent. Even Kadri can't understand much of what Halil says…and Halil has plenty to say. At that first meeting, he talked constantly. Or, rather, he announced constantly. Conversation was impossible. His "suggestions" were staccato demands: "Come," "Look," "Buy new shovel," "Geraniums here." Since we were foreigners who didn't always understand, he decided to shout his demands, in that time-honored belief that foreigners will understand if you just tell them again, louder.

Halil is a determined gardener. Even in our garden jungle, no job was too hard for him. Neighbors advised us to tear out the sorry-looking pine tree at the front of the garden. It was nearly dead. Halil differed: "No. Stays. Will grow." He nursed it back to health over several seasons. Today it is the tallest tree in the front garden.

Halil is a man who loves a project, and the most important garden project of all, in Ben's mind, was finding the perfect spot for a *çeşme* (fountain). Turks say there are three sounds essential to a man's happiness: *su sesi, kadın sesi, para sesi* (the sound of water, the sound of a woman, the sound of money). The sound of flowing water was essential to any Turkish garden. This would be no exception.

Ben and Halil became obsessed with the fountain. Ibrahim offered two *kurna*s, the marble basins used in *hamam*s. He just happened to have them in his garden; no one knew why. But he had no use for them, so they became the building blocks of the *çeşme*. Ben and Halil brought the heavy marble pieces up the hill from Ibrahim's house, and then carried them all around our garden, trying to decide where they should go, how the fountain should look, how it would work. Ben wanted to conserve water, so he needed a way to recycle the flow. This was beyond his ability to communicate with Halil, so Günhan was pulled away from the house plans to become part of the fountain planning.

She had never made a fountain before, but had seen plenty of Ottoman fountains and had wonderful ideas. They finally settled on a system putting one *kurna* above the other, with the top basin full of water, pushing a modest trickle over the side into the lower *kurna,* and somehow recycling it back to the top again. I didn't like that "somehow," but I had sworn to stay well away from this project. The spot selected was the back wall of the upper terrace, where we could hear the sound of water whenever we sat there, which we knew would be most of the time. I was foolish enough to think it was now all settled.

Once the design and placement of the fountain had been decided, Günhan suggested some decorative tiles around the base to add color and interest. She told us about a company using patterns and styles of old Ottoman tiles and producing them at reasonable prices. Their shop was in the Kapalı Çarşı, Istanbul's famed Grand Bazaar.

We had visited the bazaar many times, but had never noticed that, amidst the rugs and leather and jewelry and t-shirts, there are dozens of shops catering to ordinary Istanbul residents, not tourists. Clothing, kitchenware, sewing notions, and a host of other practical items can be found and haggled over.

From the Sirkeci ferry landing it is an easy tram ride to the Beyazıt entrance to the Grand Bazaar, that wonderfully seductive collection of more than 4,000 shops crowded along vaulted alleys and broad "avenues." We passed the familiar jewelry and leather shops with energetic salesmen trying to lure us in, but kept pace with Günhan, who was ignoring all of them as she headed directly for the tile dealer. The front of his shop had the usual tourist-quality ceramic ashtrays and dishes, but the owner led us into a small room behind the main shop where he offered tea and brought out samples of his better tiles.

There were beautiful hand-painted tulips, carnations, and other traditional Ottoman designs, most of them copies of early tiles from Iznik, the city still famous for producing these colorful ceramics. Our choice was clear: one of the designs had a white background with branches of stylized blue flowers intertwined with grapevines.

The fountain's tiles would echo the real grapes above it on our pergola. Günhan suggested that we go and walk around the bazaar for a while so she could bargain more effectively since prices rise when a "rich" foreigner is involved. They agreed to a price she was happy with, and the tiles were delivered the next day.

All seemed easy. We now had the tiles in hand. The *kurna*s were in place. A plain two-level base was fashioned out of bricks, given a smooth surface with some cement left over from other jobs, and covered with the decorative tiles. Günhan even found an old-fashioned faucet to complete the Ottoman fountain effect. Nothing else seemed to stand in the way.

But the hard part was yet to come: recycling the water. In retrospect, we remember that Günhan had told us she had absolute faith in all her *usta*s, but her usual plumber was away for several months working on a job outside Istanbul. The plumber for the fountain would be Kemal, someone she hadn't worked with before. We thought no more about it, but Kemal, whose name, ironically, means "perfection," was to provide the hard part.

Ben explained to Kemal how the fountain was to work. A submersible electric motor would power the recycling of water. Ben had seen one in a San Francisco friend's garden, but unless he wanted to submerge a transformer as well, he had to find one in Istanbul. Kemal was given some cash to buy what was needed and returned the next day with a motor. It seemed large, but he insisted that this was the only size available and set to work installing it. The island electrician, Hasan, ran a line from the house for the motor. Kemal then installed the motor, got it started, and disappeared for the rest of the day.

Günhan, Ben, and I gathered around the fountain. Was it possible? Water was going into the top *kurna*, flowing over the top, and cascading down into the lower *kurna*. Ben pulled up some chairs, told us to sit down, and went inside, returning a few minutes later with three glasses of chilled white wine. Congratulating one another on the successful completion of the Fountain Project, we clinked glasses and felt at peace with the world.

But soon the roar of the large motor was drowning out the sound of the burbling fountain. Then we noticed that the fountain wasn't actually burbling. The water flow was only intermittent. First nothing, then a sudden gush. Not exactly the Ottoman sound of water, the *su sesi,* Ben was after. Just then, the steady burbling began again, so we poured another round of wine. It was only the next day, when Günhan was in the city, that the motor did its worst.

As Ben sat happily by the fountain, the stop/gush pattern began, and then…nothing. We soon realized that the motor had burned out. Digging the packaging out of the trash, we studied the box the motor came in, but decided to wait for Günhan's return. When she arrived, she read the instructions. "Allah, Allah," she said. "This is the wrong kind of motor."

She phoned Kemal, Mr. Perfection, but he insisted there was no other motor appropriate or available. Günhan called another plumber, Mehmet, who agreed to come and have a look. With the special joy reserved for an *usta* called in to correct another *usta*'s work, he said triumphantly, "Not only is this the wrong kind of motor. He installed it upside down!"

Within a few days, another motor—same size, but correct model—was installed right side up. The water in the fountain was now flowing freely—but too quietly to compete with the sound of the motor. It wasn't entirely the fountain Ben had hoped for, but if that was the only motor available, we'd have to live with the noise. He made the best of it, but his disappointment was apparent.

Months later, Günhan triumphantly presented Ben with a tiny motor…just like the one in San Francisco, but made for Turkish current. The fountain now flows beautifully, the motor runs silently, and ivy has grown up around the sides, giving the effect of having been there for generations.

The sudden appearance of the tiny motor is part of a common phenomenon. Until the mid-1980s, Turkey imported very little. Its industry, dominated by state-owned companies, was not very creative or competitive and had little interest in acquiring new technology. Throughout the 1990s, however, things moved quickly, privatization pressed forward, and the Turkish consumer became more demanding. Some Turkish friends used to take empty suitcases on trips abroad and fill them with consumer goods impossible to find in Turkey. They no longer need to. If an item isn't available in Turkey this year, it probably will be next year. This has been true for everything from tiny submersible fountain motors to Starbucks coffee. Younger Turks don't know there is anything unusual about well-stocked shopping malls, but their parents see them as minor miracles.

******

Once the fountain was flowing, the rest of the garden work could continue. Each season brought a new focus. Some were successes, some weren't. Pruning was the first item on the agenda. The leggy rose bushes were corrected and brought back to workable size, but Halil became overzealous, doing a near fatal pruning of the hydrangeas. It took years for another flower to appear.

Next came the ivy. The fountain and wall looked quite bare, so the "right" ivy had to be found. Every variety available in greater Istanbul was studied and considered until two passed the test. Next came the year of the *minik nar* (miniature pomegranate tree), inspired by a book on Mediterranean gardens with a photo of these little trees in a charming Spanish courtyard. We now have ten of them around the garden. That led to a broader Mediterranean focus. Hours were spent deciding on just the right spot for olive and lemon trees. Friends from New York even brought us a lime tree as part of their carry-on luggage. Turkey is a wonderful citrus-growing country, but unfortunately for margarita drinkers, no climate in Turkey is right for commercial growing of the fussy lime tree. Turkish friends said our little sapling could not possibly survive the island's winter climate, but why not try?

Gardening on Heybeliada can be challenging. The climate is Mediterranean in summer, but with the Black Sea close by, winter weather can be too harsh for hot weather plants. The soil is another problem. The Princes' Islands are also known as Kızıladalar ("Red Islands"). The heavy, red soil is difficult to work. After a rain, it seems more modeling clay than soil, and, in the summer, deep cracks appear.

Ben thought he'd like a small lawn in the lower garden, near the entrance gate, and tried over and over again to make grass grow in this soil. Abject failure. By this time we had met Uğur and Inci, who live just two streets away. We can always count on good talk and helpful ideas from Uğur, a gregarious and knowledgeable tour guide and travel writer, and his wonderful wife Inci, who lovingly oversees their immaculately cared-for garden. Of particular interest now was their splendid green lawn. As we sat in their garden one evening, Ben admired their lawn and complained about his recurring failures. Uğur, a big teddy bear of a man, burst into booming laughter and said, "Of course the grass won't grow. I bring in special soil, layer it several inches deep, and use an imported grass seed you won't find anywhere in Istanbul. There's no way you can grow a lawn in *this* soil."

The red soil may be difficult, but it is amazingly fertile. A simple cutting will always take root. An avocado pit from a long-ago lunch is now a six-foot tree. The lime tree survived an unusually cold, snowy winter and was putting out new buds in April. It seems that once a plant has taken hold in this ground, it lives forever. This may explain why there were so many long-neglected survivors popping up as the garden jungle was cleared away. Aside from the lawn, there have been few garden failures, but there is one patch of ground in the lower garden where nothing, but nothing, will grow. That may be just the spot for the trumpet plant.

******

Halil worked long, hard hours despite his age, but one day, while in the city, he was hit by a bus and couldn't work for several months. When he decided he ached too much to return to work, some neighbors encouraged him to sue the bus company, but he simply shrugged, "No. Accident my fault." He no longer lives on the island, but many thriving plants are a daily reminder of him.

After Halil's departure, Ben needed another gardener. Once again, Kadri provided the solution. He had hired Mehmet for a few hours each week and could share that time with us. Mehmet, a smiling and industrious young blue-collar municipal worker, had learned some gardening techniques and was eager to expand his skills to improve his prospects. He can be seen all over the island, working in gardens, helping construction crews, moving furniture, taking on a host of odd jobs of all kinds. His hard work and agreeable nature eventually got him a promotion to maintenance man for the island's primary school. With a secure, better-paying job, he was ready to cut back a bit and informed Kadri that he could no longer work for him. But our garden's demands are more modest, so Mehmet continues to give us a few hours each week.

The garden is now past its difficult stage. Mehmet keeps it under control, leaving just enough work to keep Ben happily digging here and there. I am content with the garden as is, but Ben complains, "There's not another inch of space. I'd like a cherry tree or two, or maybe a few more herbs or vegetables, but where would I put them?"

We have learned that the small vacant lot next to our house may soon be for sale. The deed expressly forbids any building on the lot, but there would be scope for new garden obsessions. Now it is a neglected patch of land, full of brambles and bushes, too overgrown to reveal its "capabilities." If the sales rumor is true, Capability Ben may soon need to stock up again on heavy gloves and bandages.

PART II:
,BEING THERE

XII
LOST IN TIME

At the beginning of the 19th C, Istanbul was a city of walkers. At that time, the only means of transportation were walking and horse carriages.
İstanbul Ansiklopedisi (Istanbul Encyclopedia)

Once the house and garden were in reasonably good shape, we could move our attention to the more interesting side of island life: being there, enjoying what it has to offer, becoming a part of it.

There are a few magical places in the world that seem out of place, or at least out of time, with the rest of our planet. Venice is the first to come to mind. Even outside Carnival season, I wouldn't be in the least surprised to find passers-by in 18th century masks and long black cloaks. The canals and narrow streets add to the other-worldly feel. Likewise, the Princes' Islands are a step back in time. That is particularly true for the transportation, a last vestige of early 19th century Istanbul, when everyone walked or rode in horse carriages and life was free of automobiles, trams, or trains. Motor vehicles are prohibited on these islands, and a modern Istanbul resident doesn't realize how intrusive cars can be until they aren't there. When the few official service vehicles (fire, ambulance, police, garbage) roar by on Heybeliada, it is startling.

The shift to a car-less place was not much of a stretch for us, though it might be for some. Although we had always owned a car, we seemed to look for ways to avoid using it. Some people love to drive. We don't. Some people have amazing parking karma. We have none. So it was a relief to come to a place where cars are forbidden. The single best thing about Heybeliada—or any of the Princes' Islands—is this lack of cars. Modern Istanbul, like most big cities, is cursed by the combustion engine. The streets, particularly in old Stamboul, were never intended for the size or number of cars clogging them today.

Owning a car in Istanbul can be a sign of prosperity or just necessity, but, to me, *not* owning a car is the height of luxury. Taxis are plentiful and cheap and, for the more frugal, there are buses and *dolmuş* (literally, "stuffed") vans following specific routes but no fixed schedule (they depart when "stuffed" with passengers). In a city like Istanbul, it is madness to drive a car when there are so many other easy options. Living on one of the Princes' Islands, where cars are forbidden, opens a new world: going home by boat.

Sea Buses and Ferries

Four of the nine Princes' Islands are served year-round by Istanbul's graceful ferryboats and, in summer, by *deniz otobüsü* ("sea bus") catamarans that have the feel of air travel: narrow seats with tray tables, instructions to turn off cell phones, a persistent humming sound throughout the trip. The sea bus is air-conditioned and comfortable, but can't stir the soul the way the ferries do.

Before the introduction of sea buses in the late 1990s, a ferryboat (*vapur*) was the only option. These large, white vessels move slowly, silently, and gracefully through the water and still retain many of the sights, sounds, aromas, and traditions of the past. They seem to me as much a part of Istanbul's landscape as the great mosques and palaces, but there were rumors that they might be replaced by faster boats. When the rumors emerged, Istanbul residents rose up in protest. The "I want my ferries" campaign was as heartfelt as the similar "I want my radio" protests of the 1990s, when private radio stations were (unsuccessfully) outlawed.

Most *vapurs* are named for Istanbul districts or naval heroes, but I felt vicarious pride when two acquaintances had Istanbul *vapur*s renamed in their honor after their premature deaths. One was a singer and TV host beloved by the Turkish public; the other, a seismologist revered for his response to the 1999 earthquake. For a true *Istanbullu* there couldn't be a more appropriate tribute.

A *vapur* has always been one of my favorite places for people watching. Shuffled together on the hard benches are chic society women on their way to mansions on Büyükada, working men delivering furniture or vegetables or *rakı* to island merchants,

Istanbul residents looking for fresh air and picnic grounds, passengers from a mix of ethnic roots, and slender young boys in crisp white uniforms heading for the naval high school on Heybeliada. In summer, there are tourists, often in groups. They always stand out. The waiters circulating around the ship spot them and shift seamlessly into English as they pass by: "*Çay, çay*. Tea? *Çay, çay…*"

On our *vapur* rides from Sirkeci pier in old Istanbul to Heybeliada, most passengers are as silent and unhurried as the ferries themselves. They seem to sense that the relative quiet aboard a *vapur* provides the needed transition from the city to the islands. But Ben and I are always watching for our favorite *vapur* entertainment: the hawkers.

They move around the ship, selling inexpensive goods from toothbrushes to radios, hoping that no one can pass up a bargain like a kazoo-shaped gadget that extracts the juice of a lemon without cutting the fruit. It's irresistible. I've bought four of them. But the peddler's life is not an easy one. There is a delicate balance: he has to choose the right season, day, and time to find enough passengers to make his efforts worthwhile. But on an overcrowded *vapur*, potential buyers can't hear the sales pitch or see his demonstration. Some have booming voices, attract all eyes, and work hard to keep the passengers interested. Here's a sample of one of our favorites:

> "Welcome, welcome. Good afternoon and best wishes for a happy summer. No one in Turkey sells at a lower price than I do. Nobody. I offer unbelievable quality, an unbelievable opportunity. Look, dear travelers: twelve, yes twelve pencils, imported from Germany, for only…how much? In the shops, you would pay three, maybe four New Turkish Liras. But, no, I am sacrificing them at only one lira. Yes, you heard right, only one New Turkish Lira. But I haven't finished. I am also including this set of watercolors. Yes, twelve pencils plus the watercolors for only one lira. But I haven't finished. You also get these crayons. Still only one lira. But I still haven't finished. I am offering—for only one lira— twelve imported pencils, watercolors, crayons, *and* this retractable pen that writes in three colors. Who's ready to buy?"

Most buyers probably don't need the pencils and crayons, but for one New Turkish Lira (about 75 cents), it's cheap entertainment.

Some, like the pencil man, become minor celebrities, drawing the crowd's full attention and plenty of sales. Others—the Willy Lomans of the *vapur*—don't have the flair and can't sell anything. I've even seen very young children trying their luck. On one especially hot day, a small boy stopped, without a word, to fan seated passengers, hoping they might notice and buy a fan from him. Sometimes it worked.

It's rare to find a public place in Turkey without food for sale, and the *vapur* is no exception. Throughout the trip, an official *garson* or two will circulate around the ferry, selling drinks and snacks. A cold beer used to be a welcome option, but the conservative party now running the city has restricted the offerings to soft drinks. Despite their shaky legal status, non-official food sellers also make the rounds. There is usually a *simitci* selling Turkey's ubiquitous sesame bread rings, balancing the loaded tray on his head even while counting out change from his pocket. He never stops calling out, *"Simit, simit…taze, sıcak"* ("Fresh, hot *simit*s").

Vapur travelers have their favorite places to sit. Ours depends on the weather. If it's warm, we'll sit outside in the front (for some reason, it's usually less crowded than the back). If it's cold, we try to grab one of the two-seat padded benches inside. Every evening, groups of commuters get together to play cards, smoke, and drink tea on their way home to the islands. There are tables and chairs inside that would be ideal for the game, but smoking is allowed only on the open decks. They can have a table to play on or they can smoke. There is no real dilemma: the nicotine always wins, so the game is played on the wooden benches outside. A few of the older *vapur*s are three-deckers with an open top level that is perfect for camera-laden tourists. Narrow benches along the sides are the best spot for unobstructed views or for *simit* customers throwing bits of bread for the hungry seagulls, who glide next to the ferry. When the *vapur* is near the shore, a crow may land on board, look for stray scraps, then, like a flying monkey in *The Wizard of Oz*, let the wind carry him up and away.

As the *vapur* moves toward the islands, the city recedes from view and its pace and stress begin to disappear. My California childhood was mostly in the suburbs, not quite twenty miles from The City, as we always called San Francisco. Heybeliada is not really a suburb of Istanbul, and the word conjures up images quite unlike anything on the island. But one thing is the same: the separation between the city and the suburbs. Going to The City is a day's outing and a change of worlds. Moving from the noise and stress of the city to the calm and quiet of the islands needs a transition. The *vapur* is the perfect place to find it.

The pier on Heybeliada is the final transition from city to ferry and ferry to island. The scraping and thudding sounds of the gangplanks thrown from pier to ferry are the last jarring city sounds before entering the island's quiet, though the amplified announcements can be heard all the way up the hill when the wind is right (or wrong):

"This ferry will continue to Büyükada and Yalova."

"Let the departing passengers off before you try to board!"

"Buy your return ticket now. Avoid the rush at the end of the day."

The calm, silent island life seems strange at first. Istanbul is one of the noisiest cities in the world. But the contrast with the mainland—or even with the activity on board the ferry—quickly feels very soothing.

Charioteers of the Sun

Once you are on the island, you can get around by foot, bicycle, or *fayton*, a four-passenger, open carriage drawn by a brace of horses. The word *fayton* is one of those wonderful rarities in Turkish: a word the Anglophone can recognize. Introduced to Istanbul in the 19th century, the carriage took the name used in Western Europe: phaeton.

This type of open vehicle was named for Phaeton, who, in Greek mythology, demanded that his father, Helios (the Sun), let him drive the chariot of the sun for a single day. Phaeton lost control of the horses as he approached the heavens and plunged toward earth, nearly destroying the planet by fire. Zeus, exasperated by this rash youth, struck him dead with a thunderbolt, sending him tumbling into the river Eridanus. Phaeton's grief-stricken sisters wept until they were turned into poplar trees, which to this day still shed their tears, hardening them into amber.

I doubt that many of the island's *fayton* drivers know the myth or the origin of the word. It's just as well. Some of the younger drivers, who career around the island at breakneck speeds, just might try for liftoff to beat Phaeton's record. Although I've never seen a *fayton* accident, there's no guarantee.

The *fayton* is a throwback to an earlier era when they were commonly used in Istanbul. The earliest *fayton*s, in the mid-19th century were used only by the Ottoman court and its honored guests, but the use of more modest phaetons quickly spread to Istanbul residents beyond the court and lasted well into the 20th century, despite the advent of the automobile. By the mid-20th century, though, they had become obsolete everywhere except the Princes' Islands, where they are now the local version of taxi. Only the island governor has a private *fayton*.

Nearly every tourist to the islands takes a picturesque "Grand Tour" or "Short Tour" in a *fayton*. But unlike San Francisco's cable cars, which have become strictly a tourist attraction, the *fayton*s are the islands' only form of public transportation.

Today's *fayton*s look just as they have since the 19th century. Placed atop slim, oversized wheels (larger in back than in front), the four-passenger carriage has two seats facing each other and a fringed canopy on top. The driver's seat rests back-to-back with the backward-looking passenger seat. Slim metal fenders guard the wheels and protect the passengers from flying dust and mud. Old-fashioned lanterns are attached to the sides of the *fayton*, though I've rarely seen one lit. In front of the driver are the two horses, with blinders to keep them focused on the road ahead, and a "diaper" stretched below the level of the carriage to catch their leavings and avoid dirtying the streets. To keep the *fayton* on an even keel as he climbs up and down the hills, the driver has a manual braking system that needs constant attention and winding throughout the journey. The *fayton* can get up some of the hills, but not all. To get to our house, the driver has to go a long way around to avoid the steepest grades.

Most *faytons* are gaily decorated, with painted wicker seats, Easter-egg-colored cushions, and vases of flowers, usually dried or plastic. Although the *fayton* is meant for a maximum of four passengers, we have seen large families squeezed in or couples clutching a summer's worth of baggage. But we have also seen a *fayton* driver refuse to take someone he thought was too obese. Unfortunately, that person was a guest of ours. After some discussion, our friend was allowed to take a separate *fayton* by himself on the assumption that he probably didn't weigh more than two or three slimmer passengers.

Curious about the details of *fayton* life, Ben and I got into conversation with one of the older drivers, Mehmet. He explained that a *fayton* driver (*faytoncu*) is in business for himself with his own carriage and horses. There is no *fayton* boss doling out carriages to drivers-for-hire, but the *faytoncu* must complete a training course and get a license, which can be revoked if passengers complain about him or if he mistreats his horses. On Heybeliada, there are only about thirty *faytons* and a similar number of horse wagons, but they seem to be enough to serve the island's needs, even in summer when the population soars to 30,000 residents. Büyükada, as the largest and most popular island, needs well over 700 horses for its summer traffic. At the end of the season, more than 300 of those horses are sent to the Asian side of Istanbul for winter boarding. If we can learn the day of their departure, Ben and I try to be on Büyükada to watch the Felliniesque spectacle of hundreds of horses loaded onto a large, open boat, floating across the Sea of Marmara to their winter home.

A *faytoncu* works a nine-hour shift (7:00 a.m.-4:00 p.m. or 4:00 p.m.-1:00 a.m.), but is always solicitous about the horses' needs and limits. More than once, on a rainy day, a *faytoncu* has refused to take us up the hill to our house, saying that the road was too slippery to be safe for the horses. One night when we returned from the city on the last ferry, arriving on the island just after 1:00 a.m., the *faytoncu* and horses all looked exhausted at the end of their long day. As he drove the carriage along the roads to our house, the driver gently urged them on, cooing, "Come on, my beauties, just five more minutes. Then we'll go home. Come on, that's it." He knew they were tired and wished he could let them rest, but he couldn't afford to give up one last fare.

The economics of the *fayton* are a puzzle to me. The numbers don't seem to add up. Mehmet told us that it is possible to buy an older, used *fayton*, but new ones are still being made, some on Büyükada and some in a village on the Asian side of Istanbul, at a sales price equaling several thousand dollars. Once he has the carriage, a would-be *faytoncu* needs four horses; the nine-hour shift is too long for one pair. Some new drivers are from *fayton* families and can take over the foals born to family-owned horses, but for others the cost must be daunting. Shipments of hay arrive every two weeks to supply the horses' needs; for one *fayton*'s horses, the cost runs into three figures. As if this were not enough, the *fayton* itself is temperamental, causing a constant drain on the owner's resources for repairs and maintenance. To cover all these costs, the *fayton* driver must depend on the fares he can pick up—at rates that increase each year but just don't seem to add up to enough for all the expenses.

As some drivers near retirement age, there is a continuing supply of new, younger *fayton* drivers, apparently convinced that the carriages are here to stay. I hope they are right. A *fayton* ride is an irresistible tourist attraction, something unique to the islands. For residents, the *fayton* is essential transportation. From time to time, new island residents try to introduce other forms of transportation, and island officials sometimes use the municipal vehicles for their personal convenience. Luckily, a vigilant citizens group nips these ideas in the bud. If cars, motorcycles, scooters, loud music, or other city intrusions come, the islands will no longer have the special character that has made them something unique for more than 2,000 years.

XIII
WALK THE WALK

The sum of the whole is this: walk and be happy; walk and be healthy.
                       Charles Dickens

Other than *fayton* or bicycle, the only way to get around the island is on foot. I've been a walker all my life. For me, a perfect day has always included several hours on foot, preferably in a big city where I can observe the people and architecture, finally stopping for a good meal somewhere. Nature walks have never had more than limited appeal, but the island's quiet, car-free paths and roads, within easy reach of cafes or my own garden, are now my preferred habitat.

Some of our overseas guests, accustomed to driving even the shortest distance, take a while to adjust to this, but Heybeliada's clean air, forest trails, and sea vistas are irresistible. They can seduce even the most reluctant walker.

Everyone on the island walks. Some are rushing to the early morning *vapur* to get to work in the city, stopping only for a newspaper to read on the ferry or a hot *poğaça*, a flaky cheese-filled pastry, to serve as breakfast. Evening strollers do a form of *paseo,* going nowhere in particular, but just ready for a walk in the evening air. Some prefer the seaside and its teashops and ice cream stands; others wander around their own neighborhoods, stopping as they see friends, hoping for an impromptu cocktail party.

We are usually among the morning fitness walkers taking the route around the perimeter of the island. Heybeliada has not escaped the modern obsession with exercise. There are always a few joggers and walkers in full workout regalia, and even some of the village women in traditional dress can be seen sporting brand-new Adidas or Nikes as they saunter along the road on a not very aerobic morning stroll. On weekends, hiking clubs head into less traveled parts of the island, and hordes of picnickers descend on any beautiful summer weekend, walking from the dock to the far side of the island, settling into their favorite picnic area or beach.

But my favorite walkers are what you might call:

A Different Breed of Street Musician

At first I didn't notice these people among the many kinds of island walkers, but then I became aware of someone calling:

"Sebastian? Sebastian?"

Each evening at about the same time, as I sat under the grape arbor with a glass of chilled white wine, savoring the soft evening air, I could hear this repeated cry. No, not a cry, a question. "Sebastian?"

Who, I wondered, is that man walking through the streets every evening, calling out to Sebastian? Why doesn't Sebastian ever answer? One evening Kadri was with us when I heard the call, so I asked if he had any idea what it was.

"Ah," he explained, "that's Ramazan. He pushes his vegetable cart through the neighborhood every evening, asking, 'Does anyone want vegetables?' ('*Sebze isteyen?*' as Ramazan said it, sounded just like 'Sebastian.')."

This was my introduction to the world of Heybeliada's strolling street merchants. Reminiscent of the songs of street sellers in 19th century London ("Who will buy my pretty lavender?"), these cries are still heard in some Turkish towns and have a language all their own. In modern mainland Istanbul neighborhoods, such calls have mostly disappeared or been replaced by loudspeakers on trucks, but they are still a vibrant part of island life, slicing through the customary silence as the merchants move up and down the hilly streets. Some are strolling merchants; others, with heavy containers of water or gas, use horse wagons. But all belong to the same tradition.

We listen for the specific pitch and tune for each one. During a Heybeliada summer, the most frequently heard is the cry of the water seller or *sucu*. Most people don't drink the tap water. When the island's water pipes were replaced recently, samples of the old and new pipes were put on display. One look at the encrusted old pipes easily explained why people buy bottled water.

The *sucu* makes several rounds a day, heaving nineteen-liter (nearly five-gallon) replacement jugs of drinking water into his customers' houses and removing the empties. In the *sucu* business, no two merchants sell the same brand of water. Each has his own wagon and calls out his own variation on the theme. Our man has an emphatic, monosyllabic "SU" ("water"). A rival *sucu* offers a gentler, almost tentative "*sucu*" that recalls a doorbell's "ding-dong." Another accents the second syllable, "*suCU*." But we know which is our man and can ignore the others.

Everyone on Heybeliada depends on these carts for water and gas. Municipal natural gas, piped in from the mainland, has just come to the islands, but until now everyone used gas canisters for cooking and water heating. The leading company is called Aygaz, which would have to translate as "moon gas." It seems an odd name for a gas company, but the moon looms large in the Turkish imagination and language. We know people with names like "First Moon" (Ilkay) or "From the Moon" (Aydan) or "Moonlight" (Aynur). There are surnames like "Moonrise" (Aydoğdu), and a beautiful woman can be described as being like a full moon. The plant we call a sunflower is a "moonflower" (*ayçiçek*) in Turkish. Some say this interest in the moon goes back to pre-Islamic animist tradition, but others have never given it a moment's thought.

Whatever the reason for its name, Aygaz is the leading gas company. Their heavy canisters weigh more than thirty pounds and hold enough gas to run a stove for quite a while or to supply hot water for a surprisingly large number of showers. They are far too heavy to carry up the hill, so the *sucu* brings them along with the water jugs in a horse cart. In Istanbul neighborhoods where natural gas is not universal, flatbed trucks transport the gas canisters and play a recording of a distinctive tune known to be the Aygaz theme. It just isn't the same.

Other merchants stroll by the house throughout the day, each with a different sound and call. On the basso end of the scale, but with three full syllables to work with, the *eskici*, or junk collector, is easily distinguished from the *sucu*. His call hints at the opening of Beethoven's Symphony No. 5: he begins with *"Es-ki"* on the same note, then down to a minor chord for the *"-ci"* to finish off. It's not quite Beethoven—it's a note short—but that shift to the minor key always brings the Fifth to mind.

There are no women making the island rounds and, as far as I can recollect, no tenors. The vocal range remains pretty much basso to baritone. Tempos can range from the *sucu*'s adagio to the vowel-swallowing, staccato *"Smit! Smit!"* from the seller of Turkey's favorite street snack, the sesame bread ring called *simit*. Neighborhood children amuse themselves for hours pretending to be merchants and imitating the calls. They also play *fayton*, with the youngest ones pressed into service as the horses.

Though not really in the same category, the mail carrier is part of the street calls. Summer residents usually live here only three months of the year, so they don't get much mail on the island. The mail carrier's load can't be very interesting for him. When he has something for us, he always calls out *"Günaydın"* ("Good morning") or *"Postacı"* ("mailman") just to let us know he's leaving something. He seems pleased over anything more interesting than utility bills, and an order from Amazon.com can make his day.

Some street merchants make a brief appearance, then disappear for months. When artichokes are plentiful, a young man offers sacks of perfectly cleaned and prepared artichoke bottoms—his only merchandise—but we don't see him again until the next season. In spring, as people begin to get their homes in order after the winter, a knife sharpener walks the neighborhoods, providing his services with a fairly primitive sharpening stone and manual grinder on a small pushcart. For a year or two, an industrious upholsterer came to the island in the summer and hit a mother lode. He carried no merchandise, but called out his availability for work and would do an estimate on the spot. We were finally able to get those Art Deco chairs recovered. He was the first upholsterer on the island in a long time, but he must have run through the potential customers and moved on to the next island. He has disappeared and his workshop in the village is empty.

Except for water and Aygaz, we don't really need most of the things being sold, but we buy whenever we can, just to encourage them. It's a throwback to an earlier era, but a pleasant addition to the sounds and traditions of the island.

The Grand Tour

Heybeliada is a compact island, unlike its much larger neighbor, Büyükada. In an hour or so, we can walk the *fayton*'s "grand tour" route. This is the best way to give our visitors a sense of the island. Starting on the main street (Refah Şehitleri Caddesi), we point out some of the island's best architecture, stately 19th and early 20th century wooden villas. Then we can admire Çiçekli Dağ ("flowered mountain"), a steep stairway street with trees and flowers along the stairs and lovely wooden houses on either side. Passing the elegantly restored Halki Palas Hotel, we continue past a few new apartment houses, where open-air teashops or *gazino*s used to be, and then face a fork in the road at the upper campus of the naval high school. If our visitors are not used to walking, we take a shortcut to the left, cutting across the middle of the island, along a road known as "Lovers' Lane" (Aşıklar Yolu). Its forestland and beautiful views make it a favorite spot for trysting couples; some island friends tell us of hiding in the trees when they were children to spy on the lovers.

But for our walk, we prefer to take our visitors on the main road around the edge of the island, into the forest, with paths here and there leading down to beaches. Through the trees, other islands are visible: Burgaz and Kaşık islands just below and two tiny islands, Yassı ("flat") and Sivri ("pointed"), in the distance. There may be a few other walkers, a bicyclist or two, horse carriages, wagons, or even a few horses or cows wandering freely on their own. The scent of the pine trees is exhilarating and the light changes throughout the day, playing on the water and filtering through the trees. There is only nature here, sea views on one side, and paths into the lush green hills on the other. This natural setting was used—and elephants and monkeys imported—for a strange 1952 Turkish film called *Tarzan in Istanbul*.

We continue on past a promontory with stables for the *fayton* and delivery wagon horses. In the early morning, when few others are stirring, we sometimes see the drivers standing up in the wagons, galloping their horses down to the waterside to pick up arriving merchandise for the first deliveries of the day. It's a mundane chore, but they always look dashing.

As the road curves toward the bay (Çam Limanı), a small sign, *Terk-i-Dünya* (a nice double meaning of "land's end" or "leaving the world behind"), points to a dirt path leading through the trees to the small but meticulously maintained Arsenios Monastery, perched on a precipice and named for the founding priest, considered a saint by both Turks and Greeks on the island. During the summer season, a monk is usually there, but in winter, a family of caretakers will let us into the small church and offer a glass of tea.

We stop next at the viewing platform just above Çam Limanı. There will often be a *fayton* driver resting his horses while the passengers photograph the bay and the yachts moored there. Cyclists, too, find this a good halfway point for a rest. Our road then descends to the bay and back up again to the old sanatorium, now closed. The southern side of the island is mostly a military (naval) zone (No Entry! Military Zone! No Photos or Filming Allowed!) with housing, harbor, and school facilities. The Greek and Turkish cemeteries are side by side on the hill, and, on a sharp slope facing Büyükada, a small monastery sits near the ruins of a tomb (Süslü Mezar) built by a 19th century Greek to honor the memory of his wife. It is a mini-Taj Mahal, in intent if not in style.

As we approach the ferry landing, a small park faces the naval school. A lovely oasis of shade on a hot summer day, the park contains a bust of Yesari Asim Arsoy (1896-1992), who wrote the famous *"Biz Heybeli'de…"* song about the bygone days of evening revelries at Çam Limanı. It is worth a short pause to admire the wooden houses nearby and to smile at the statue of the dapper Mr. Arsoy. Both are relics of the island's golden age.

This one-hour walk is the best way to introduce our visitors to the island. It takes in Heybeliada's natural beauty and architectural gems, evokes the former Greek presence, and suggests the importance of the Navy on the island. I never tire of it, and it never looks the same twice. The light, the water, the clouds, the greenery are ever changing. We inspect the number and size of boats on the water, and gauge the progress of the tourist season by the number of picnickers we pass on the road.

The size and pace of Heybeliada are just right for strolling. This is not a place for hurry or stress. Only an arriving ferry or sea bus causes islanders to quicken their pace. One day, on my way to Kadri and Nilgün's house, I somehow fell into a city-like brisk walk. Old habits die hard. An old man down the street watched me for a moment, shook his head, and said, "What can you be hurrying to? What could be so urgent and important?" What, indeed?

XIV
SALTLESS SOUP MEETS ÇOLUK ÇOCUK

A man without children is like a soup without salt.
Turkish proverb

According to this Turkish proverb, Ben and I would seem to be saltless soup. We have no children of our own, but our life in Turkey, including on Heybeliada, hasn't been salt-free. Turkish children and young people have always been a part of our experience in this country. That's not surprising. The majority of the Turkish population is under twenty-five years old.

The term *çoluk çocuk* can't be translated precisely. *Çocuk* means "child." *Çoluk* is not really a word, but this Turkish rhyme gives the same notion as Zorba's "full catastrophe": married with children and all the complications they bring. *Çoluk çocuk* is a central feature of life in Turkey. On the island, if there is a single obstacle to attaining a peaceful life, it may be *çoluk çocuk*.

Our teaching experience in Turkey was at the university level, so we had little contact with younger Turkish kids until we moved to Heybeliada. The street in front of our island house offers a flat area in this hilly part of the island, as well as one of the few streetlights. It is the ideal place for a soccer game. It's about the only place in the immediate neighborhood. Most island families can't afford the sports club on the other side of the island; members are mostly the affluent Istanbul families who spend the summer here. As a public service, the club offers swimming lessons to non-members' children, but what the year-round island kids really want to do is play ball—soccer or volleyball, but mostly soccer—using whatever space they can find. One space they love is the one right in front of our house.

Soccer is not a quiet game, and one of the boys, with the unexpected name Yağmur ("rain"), has the loudest and most distinctive voice of any child since George "Foghorn" Winslow. We always know when he's part of the game. At first the noise of the games seemed random and unpredictable, but experience revealed a pattern. Somehow noise is more tolerable when it is a little more predictable. Just as the seagulls are more clamorous at certain seasons and hours, just as the mosque's *muezzin* recites the call to prayer on a five-times-per-day schedule printed in the newspaper, so too there is a rhythm and (limited) predictability to the games.

Morning is nearly always quiet until 10:30 or 11:00 when the smallest children come out with their wagons and toy cars. The rattling wheels and the shrieks of delight as they career down the hill will continue only a half-hour or so. By then these tykes have gotten tired and bored with dragging the heavy toys back up the hill again.

The next wave is usually a pre-adolescent group of boys and girls. They have more stamina, but do more talking than playing. From time to time a ball gets kicked around, but their hearts aren't really in it. They're just waiting for their mothers to call them in for lunch.

Then, after lunch, come the older boys, voices long since changed, displaying a little more attitude than the little ones. They play serious soccer for a while, but with the limited attention span of teenagers anywhere they soon decide it's too hot or too boring, and move on to their computer games. After dinner, it seems to be a mixed group of all ages, mostly hanging around, sometimes playing soccer. On a cool summer night, the games can last until midnight.

The kids were pleasant, but the games and noise got to be too much. I spoke with some island officials about opening some playground space to the island kids. It should be easier to shoo them away if they have someplace better to go.

"Nothing available," they said.

"How about the high school playing field," I countered.

"Not under my authority. Belongs to the Ministry of Education."

"How about that large field near the yacht bay?"

"Not my authority. Belongs to the Ministry of Forestry."

At moments like this I remember I live in the former Byzantium.

Impasse. I knew that the very worst solution would be to go onto the balcony and yell at the kids to be quiet. There is no point becoming The Bad Guy, and, in any case, there is the problem of being eloquently angry in a foreign language.

I decided to try a friendlier method. I approached the children, who were terrifically amused by my strange accent and agog at the idea of a conversation with The Foreigner. I tried to win them over with reason and concern. Like most Turkish children, they are good-natured and trained to be respectful to adults. They heard me out. They agreed with me. They promised to do everything in their power to ensure that we were not disturbed by their games. It worked for about twenty-four hours. Then back to Step One.

I decided to take a more Turkish approach. One day, as the kids settled in for the evening, draped around our front gate as usual, I explained that sitting in front of our gate would henceforth be *yasak* ("forbidden"). I didn't actually forbid the soccer game, since it is, after all, a public street, but at least I could ask them to move someplace past our property. This seemed to have some effect, though Arzu, the oldest and therefore de facto leader, pointed out that they come here because everyplace else is *yasak*. Aha!

I added our house to their *yasak* list. All was settled and agreed. They all solemnly swore that they would no longer sit at our entrance gate. Ben and I spent the evening at Kadri and Nilgün's house, telling them optimistically that we would now be free of the problem. Kadri just laughed. "Can I tell you something? I played football in front of that house when I was young; my son played there when he was a child. Those kids' grandchildren will also be playing in front of that house. Forget about it."

Returning home at the end of the evening, we saw most of the kids farther down the block, but Yağmur was sitting at our gate. "I thought we agreed," I reminded him. "Did you forget?" Expecting an argument, I was amazed to see him slink away, saying apologetically, "I forgot. I'm so used to sitting here."

Ah! *Yasak* works. But it would have to be used sparingly. All went well for a few days until, returning home one afternoon, Ben and I discovered a city bench placed across an unused entrance to our garden. Holding back a chuckle at their chutzpah and wondering where they found the bench and how they got it up the hill, I steeled myself for the next scene. This could not go unchallenged.

They swore ignorance and innocence, then helped us move the bench up the street where it would block no one's property and, I hoped, might draw them well away from our house. Arzu, too, wasn't going to let this one pass. She began to complain again about the lack of play areas on the island.

"What about the high school sports field," I asked.

"*Yasak*," she replied.

I told her of my fruitless conversations with the island authorities. We began to understand each other. A woman passing by took interest, got the gist, shrugged, and said not unkindly, "What do you expect? Kids have no rights."

I stopped by the high school later that day. A fortyish bearded man appeared as I looked at the playing field and, responding to my questions, said, yes, he is a school official, and, no, he has no objections to letting the kids play here. "As long as they don't break any windows." When the kids gathered that evening for their game, I told them the schoolyard was no longer *yasak*.

The following day, Arzu went to see if this was true, then asked if I could talk with the school about providing a volleyball and net. She saw her new role as volleyball coach to the younger kids. Knowing that would push the school too far, I decided to look for a volleyball next time I was in the city. It seemed a minor investment for restoring peace and quiet.

******

What we hadn't thought through, of course, is that children grow up. Arzu and Yağmur and the others suddenly grew up one year and haven't been around in a long time. When I see Arzu now, she's with her mother or aunts or older teenage girls. She has become a young woman. We'll probably hear of her wedding before long.

Meanwhile, just as Kadri predicted, a new generation of kids discovered that the space in front of our house is nice and flat, pretty well shaded, equipped with a streetlight, and just about perfect for games and hanging out any time of the night or day.

As years have passed and we have spent more time on the island, the unlikely has happened. The sounds have become part of the background now, seeming no more extraordinary than the cry of the seagulls. Someone seems to have put more salt in our soup.

XV
TALK THE TALK

I am fond of the Turks.... It is my special intention, as an exercise in mortification, to learn the Turkish language.

Angelo Giuseppe Roncalli (later Pope John XXIII)
Papal nuncio in Istanbul, 1934-44

Learning the language, they say, is the way to understand a country. It provides clues about the culture; it opens doors. Maybe so, but an expatriate living in central Istanbul can survive pretty well without much Turkish. There, as in most of the world, English is the dominant second language. But on an island in the Sea of Marmara, learning the language isn't optional.

The Turkish language is not an easy one for Anglophones. I had studied French and some Italian without any serious mental scars, but soon found that Turkish is a very different proposition. Unlike romance languages, Turkish offers few cognates, few free rides to the struggling learner. There are just enough French and English borrowings to ward off total despair. For many years, linguists said Turkish was related to Finnish and Hungarian. All three are devilishly hard to learn and all share certain grammatical quirks, but experts now classify Turkish as a Ural-Altaic language, in the same family as Mongolian. This makes more sense. The Turkic people originally came from Central Asia. I have been told that Japanese and Korean are among the easiest languages for Turks to learn. No wonder Anglophones have problems.

Modern Turkish thrives on suffixes. There sometimes seems no limit to them. Turkish proofreaders and translators are paid by the keystroke, not by the word. One word in Turkish can translate into several in another language, and Turks love to confound foreigners with what is alleged to be their longest word:

Çekoslovakyalılaştıramadıklarımızdanmısınız?

("Are you one of those whom we were unable to make into a

Czechoslovak?")

The word is now politically outdated and always was, in my opinion, enigmatic. But it shows what suffixes in Turkish can lead to. Most Anglophones who make some effort to learn Turkish give up in the early stages. The syntax is just too puzzling. In fact, if you hang in there for a bit, efforts are amply rewarded.

I think of Turkish as being like algebra. It takes a while to get used to the rules, but once you know them, you can rely on them. Turkish grammar has virtually no exceptions and only one irregular verb. There are no genders, and Turks who speak otherwise superb English often mix up "he" and "she." Our first Turkish teacher liked to say, "The good news about learning Turkish: there are no genders. The bad news: that's the *only* good news."

Actually, the other good news is that modern Turkish is easy to read. Ottoman Turkish (*Osmanlıca*) was written in Arabic script, singularly unsuited to its needs. Turkish contains sounds not found in Arabic and relies heavily on vowels and vowel harmony, which cannot be rendered well in Arabic script. Thanks to Atatürk, however, Turkish has, since 1928, been written with a phonetic Latin alphabet, including a few invented letters to accommodate Turkish sounds (see the Turkish Pronunciation notes at the beginning of this book).

There were good reasons for the change. At the end of the Ottoman Empire, the literacy rate in Turkey was less than 10%. There was a huge gulf between the formal, literary Ottoman court language, filled with words of Arabic and Persian origin, and the simpler spoken Turkish of the people. To aid literacy efforts and as another way to move away from the Ottoman past, Atatürk's reform simplified and Westernized the alphabet and purged the language of many Arabic and Persian words, substituting common Turkish words or, in many cases, inventing new ones.

The tactic worked and literacy rates rose quickly. But it also meant that in the new Turkey, even educated citizens would soon be unable to read their own history. Even if texts are transliterated from the Arabic to the Latin alphabet, they are filled with words that are now unfamiliar. In recent years, as part of a revival of interest in the Ottoman past, the young generation of Turks has become interested in recapturing the richness of *Osmanlıca*. Istanbul's Tarih Vakfı (History Foundation), a non-profit organization working to create better understanding and appreciation of Turkey's past, now offers evening lessons in *Osmanlıca*. To attract students and to indicate this is not just for scholars, the course is titled "I Want to Read My Grandfather's Letters."

Atatürk's reforms were a boon for foreigners trying to learn modern Turkish: with a phonetic written language there is no problem reading or pronouncing. Of course, it doesn't necessarily mean you'll understand what you've been able to say, but sometimes there are unexpected freebies. Turkish has borrowed some words from French and English, often for things that were brought in from the West and for which there was no good Turkish equivalent. Since the words are written phonetically, they don't immediately look like the foreign words. In my earliest days in Turkey, I would look at signs as I walked along, sounding out the words. Once in a while, something would register. As I sounded out *kuaför*, for example, I realized it was "coiffeur." In shops, when I struggled to find a way to ask for a light bulb or a corkscrew, I would feel a great relief when it turned out to be "*ampul*" or "*tirbuşon*," French words (*ampoule; tire-bouchon*) I already knew and could remember.

There seem to be certain categories of words that came from French (older, often low-tech terms dating from the days when French was the dominant second language), others from English (computer terminology is full of English borrowings). Now when I'm at a loss for a word, I'll try French or English. Sometimes it works, but only about as often as Google's "I'm feeling lucky."

An embarrassing problem is that the mind is a trickster. When you have some knowledge of more than one foreign language, you can count on the one you *don't* want to pop out. My Turkish is usually at its best when I'm in France and vice versa. This transference can cause problems. One day in a Turkish pharmacy, I wanted to buy dental floss and, remembering only that the Turkish term is "tooth string," I confidently asked for "*diş fili*." Unfortunately, *fil* is the French, not Turkish word, for "string." It took me a while to realize why the pharmacist looked puzzled. Why was this woman asking for a "tooth elephant"?

Yes, learning Turkish takes a while. English and Turkish have different learning curves. People can speak acceptable English fairly quickly, but it takes years to master the exceptions, contradictions, and just plain illogical quirks of English. How do non-native speakers ever get prepositions straight?

In Turkish the initial leap is longer. The baby-talk level lasts for a long time, but once you can put together these strange strings of suffixes in what seems to us "reverse" order, then you're on your way. After that, it's mostly a matter of memorizing vocabulary, but that, too, has its pitfalls.

Not counting technical or scientific terms, English has upwards of 500,000 words. Because so much depends on suffixes, it's harder to give an accurate figure for Turkish, but my Turkish-English dictionary claims to have 100,000 entries. The actual number of root words is much, much smaller. A woman who developed an online Turkish dictionary told me her site contains only 5,000 words. That would seem to limit nuances in Turkish, and, indeed, there are many words that seem to serve too many purposes. Turks use the same word, for example, for "worried" and "curious" (*meraklı*). Another word serves for "sinewy," "nervous," or "bad-tempered" (*sinirli*). As in French, the same word is used for "stranger" and "foreigner" (*yabancı*). And yet, there are sometimes Turkish words for things that English sees no need to be particular about. Why, for example, should Turkish have a specific word for "immune to snake bite" (*şerbetli*)? And why should that word do triple duty, also meaning "incorrigible" and "watered by manure tea"? And what *is* "manure tea" anyway?

The main problem with learning Turkish is, again, those suffixes. Each suffix adds another layer of meaning—it may shift the tense, the modifier, or the word itself. If you aren't looking or listening carefully, you can miss the meaning completely. And spelling definitely counts. In this thrifty, phonetic language, each letter may create a new word or meaning, so remembering which is which can be confusing or sometimes embarrassing. Look, for example, at *haletmek, halletmek, halleşmek, hallenmek, halelenmek.* It's easy to confuse one for the other, but their wildly different meanings are, respectively, to depose a ruler, to find a solution, to have a heart-to-heart talk, to hassle a woman, to form a halo.

Small slips are easy to fall into, and there are dozens of stories that may or may not be apocryphal. I am doubtful about some that I have heard again and again. They are practically urban legends. But for one of them you first need to know that Turkish is possibly unique in having an infallible way of attracting a waiter's attention. U.S. diners can listlessly call out "Excuse me" or use the waiter's name (at least in California restaurants, his first words will have been, "Hi, I'm Josh and I'll be your server tonight."). Whatever we do, the American waiter usually remains deaf and blind. In France, a waiter will ignore anyone so rude as to call out "*garçon*" and he certainly won't have revealed his name, so you're back to "Excuse me." In Turkey, however, there is a magic phrase, *Bakar mısınız?*, that makes any waiter snap immediately to attention. The verb can mean either "Would you look over here?" or "Would you come and take care of us?" I've never been sure which meaning is intended, but either one suits the need.

A student of Turkish wanted to try this magical phrase. One night, at a crowded fish restaurant, she had her chance. The harried waiter was cleaning off a table across the room, but glanced up just long enough for her to catch his eye. She got only one letter wrong as she called out, "*Bekar mısınız?*" ("Are you a bachelor?").

Luckily for the language learner, Turkey is a supportive place. A French waiter would not be amused, but after the initial shock the Turkish waiter would regain his composure, realize she wasn't proposing marriage, and come to see what was needed. Unlike the French, most Turks are delighted whenever a foreigner makes an effort to speak their language. A simple *merhaba* ("hello") wins friends. Not many foreigners speak Turkish, so it is an event when one tries. Uttering more than two or three words of Turkish will elicit polite exclamations about what wonderful Turkish you speak. One day while Ben and I were waiting at the ferry dock at Sirkeci, someone spotted us as foreigners and wanted to practice his English. We just said, *"Merhaba."* He exclaimed, "Oh, you speak Turkish!" and went off into a long monologue in Turkish, during which we simply nodded and smiled. At the end, he complimented us on our extraordinary Turkish though we'd never said another word.

You know that you are actually beginning to learn the language when a Turkish friend starts to correct you. That's a sign that you've made enough progress to merit serious encouragement. When we first came to the island, Ibrahim spoke to us in English or French, sometimes giving us the Turkish word at the same time. Now he is merciless. He won't speak anything but Turkish and corrects our mistakes. It is very flattering.

******

Learning a language does provide clues about a new culture, but it also reveals quirks of one's own language. Just as Americans prefer a "let's-get-down-to-business" approach, while Turks want to take time to establish a personal relationship, so, too, the languages reflect differences.

Unlike Americans, Turks are not comfortable with using first names right away. Formality requires a traditional honorific after the first name—*Bey* for men or *Hanım* for women. It was not until 1934, as part of Atatürk's reforms, that Turks began to use surnames. "Mehmet Bey" or "Zeynep Hanım" was, and still is, as formal as our saying "Mr. Smith" or "Ms. Jones." This is wonderful. When I'm unable to remember someone's surname, it doesn't matter. But leaving off the "*Bey*" or "*Hanım*" with someone you don't know well is a bit like using the familiar "*tu*" too soon in French. It may seem odd that a Turk might take offense at being called Zeynep rather than Zeynep Hanım, but there is a wide chasm between the two.

Family life is central to Turkish culture and its terminology is used to soften this formality. We have no middle ground between "Joe" and "Mr. Smith," but when a Turk isn't yet ready for first-name familiarity, he may address another man as *ağabeyi* (contracted to *abi*), the word for "elder brother," or a woman as *abla* ("elder sister"). Saying "Mehmet Abi" or "Zeynep Abla" shows respect but also a bit of warmth. A younger person might say *"abi"* or *"abla"* to a slightly older or higher-ranking colleague. Merchants say it to their customers, and small children to teenagers or adults. But, just as French women dread the day strangers start calling them *madame* instead of *mademoiselle*, a Turkish woman happy to be called *abla* may resent being called *teyze* ("aunt"), a term used only for, as the French say, "women of a certain age."

******

Modern Turkish is quite different from the pre-republican *Osmanlıca*, but old traditions of hospitality and graciousness still permeate the language. American directness, if literally translated, can sound abrupt or even rude in Turkish. Ottoman etiquette required a show of modesty, if not inferiority, when speaking to someone of the same or higher social rank. Even today, if a Turk is trying to make you understand his point, but sees that you are just not getting it, he won't ask, "Did you understand?" That might suggest that you are at fault. The Turk will ask, "Was I able to explain?" Even the Turkish version of "Happy Birthday" is designed to honor the celebrant: *İyi ki doğdun* ("How good it is that you were born").

Turks have come a long way from the formalized, ceremonial speech of the Ottoman court, but a welcome holdover is the existence of the "right" phrase for nearly any occasion. Americans fret over what should be said at a funeral or when someone has received bad news. We are often awkward and sometimes inadvertently offensive. Turks, however, always have a phrase that is expected and sufficient. No more, no less is required, expected, or even wanted. A Turkish friend who worked as a journalist in Washington DC told me this was the hardest part of living in the United States. He kept looking for those phrases in English and didn't understand how we do without them. Now that I've seen how useful they are, I wonder, too.

They do take up the slack in many situations. A simple *geçmiş olsun* ("may it pass") can show your compassion for anything from a headache to bankruptcy. Dentists and manicurists end their work with *geçmiş olsun* to announce that any discomfort is over. If you call the police to report a robbery, they will end the call with *geçmiş olsun*.

On the other hand, Turks have a phrase to wish you happiness in any new endeavor. If you have a new house, may you live there happily (*güle güle oturun*). If you have a new coat, may you wear it with joy (*güle güle giyin*). If you have a new job, may you enjoy working there (*güle güle çalışın*). The phrase is so automatic that its use sometimes becomes inventive. As our housekeeper leaves at the end of her work, she smiles and says *güle güle kirletin* ("Enjoy dirtying it") in anticipation of our slovenly preparation for her return the next week.

Other phrases are more puzzling. "What about funerals?" I asked a Turkish friend. "I never know what to say."

"The single best thing to say to the family of the deceased," she insisted, "is *Başınız sağ olsun* or *Başsağlığınız olsun*. The literal translation is 'May your head be healthy.'" I thought it seemed strange, even a little heartless, to ignore the deceased and wish the survivor better luck. "No," she said, "that is what you say. No more, no less. The closest thing in English might be 'The king is dead. Long live the king.' The idea is that the survivor shouldn't give up or despair; life must go on." Whatever the origin of the phrase, it is an improvement over our stumbling efforts in English to find something comforting to say.

There are dozens of these phrases, and using them is almost like a cheat sheet to get through conversations without having to worry about grammar, syntax, or even vocabulary. It is probably possible to have an entire conversation consisting only of these set phrases. But living on Heybeliada has forced us to use Turkish far more than we might in the city. Evenings with some of our fluent English-speaking friends are the exception, but mostly our island life is in Turkish, though I still can't claim the proficiency I'd like to have.

Somehow it never occurred to me that any of the merchants or other year-rounders might speak English. They all know we're Americans, but none of them has ever indicated any knowledge of English. It was only when friends from San Francisco came to visit that the truth came out.

They had gotten up very early one morning and gone off for a walk around the island. When they returned, Joanna and Lawrence told us about stopping at one of the cafés, drinking cappuccino and talking with the owner. We were amazed at how they had stumbled into this. Not only had they instinctively gone to the only café on Heybeliada that serves cappuccino, but they had found, we thought, possibly the only English speaker, too. When we said as much to them, they couldn't understand. No, they said, they'd been speaking English to all the merchants…and paying them with cash dollars, too. Who knew?

XVI
TO THE CITY

... What's in Istanbul?
There's Istanbul in Istanbul.
Cahit Irgat (1916-1971), "Istanbul"

Every small place or group has its own quirks of language or idiom. Heybeliada is no exception. On the island, if you go downhill to the shopping area, you are *aşağıda* ("down below"). If you go to the Asian side, you are *karşıda* ("on the opposite side") and, though the islands are part of the Istanbul municipality, when you take the ferry to the European shore, you are going *Istanbul'a* ("to Istanbul").

For an island that once was 90% *Rum* (Greek), that usage is probably appropriate. The name "Istanbul" came from the Greek *eis tin polis*, meaning "to the city." The proximity of the city is the icing on the cake. We have the island's serenity and beauty when we want it, but when our urban side gets restive, we also have everything Istanbul can offer—and only a short boat ride away. The ferries start early and end late, so we can easily get to Istanbul's restaurants, arts festivals, and friends' houses.

Our visitors from abroad spend most of their time in Sultanahmet, site of the main monuments and museums. But we try to get them to other areas as well. Our *Istanbullu* friends are justly proud of their city. Though they grumble about galloping population growth and urban sprawl, they can't imagine living anywhere else. This is the cultural, media, educational, and commercial center of the country, with more to do and see than any one person can manage. Some of our *Istanbullu* friends admit that if they are away for more than two weeks, they fall into a melancholy funk. Kadri, in all good faith, asked why we sometimes spend weeks or months in San Francisco. "Is there anything to *do* there?" he inquired quite sincerely.

We, too, have become Istanbul boosters, always ready to show off our chosen city. Our foreign visitors, on the other hand, seem to expect Istanbul to be a tableau of Orientalism clichés, pure 1001 Nights. A couple of days into a visit from a Manhattanite friend, we noticed that Mike, an avid photographer, had not yet used his camera except to photograph the ferryboat.

"Are you having problems with your camera?" we asked. "There's a good repair shop you can take it too."

"No, no, it's fine," he said, but it was clear that something was wrong.

Then we understood. He wasn't seeing what he came for: no camels, no dancing bears, not enough headscarves, and not a single chador. Well, he had spent a Fulbright year in rural North Africa, so we could even forgive him when he spotted some gypsies selling flowers in Istanbul and, snapping photo after photo, said with glee, "Look! Bedouins!"

Bedouins? In Istanbul?

OK, we thought, let's take him on a tour. We'll go to the most traditional or exotic place we can find—as long as his slide show back home *also* depicts Istanbul as Turkey's booming business, arts, and media center. By all means, photograph the headscarves, but don't forget the camera as you stroll along the boulevards packed with hip young people.

As we planned our itinerary, we thought Mike should have some background, so we invited a couple of neighbors, Istanbul natives and fluent English speakers, to help give Mike a better picture of today's Istanbul. We sat on our terrace, looking at the sprawling new suburbs of Asian Istanbul, as our neighbors, white wine or *rakı* in hand, warmed to their task.

"Over the last generation," they explained to Mike, "Istanbul has been a magnet for Turks from all corners of this country of more than seventy million. The population of Istanbul mushroomed from under five million in 1980 to well over ten million in 2000 and maybe fifteen million today. That's only a guess; no one really knows for sure and the last census estimate seemed far too low. Istanbul is growing twice as fast as the rest of Turkey."

We knew we could prove that to Mike when we got into town. New construction, trying to keep pace with growth, mingles everywhere with the layers of history along the Bosphorus.

"This is an old city in terms of history, but a very young city in terms of population," they continued. "Young people swarm to the city for jobs and excitement. This is a young country: more than two-thirds of Turkey's population is under thirty-five, and nearly 80% of those moving to Istanbul since 1985 have been under twenty-five."

But our longtime *Istanbullu*s were less enthusiastic about the arrival of indigent villagers from southeastern Turkey. These people, fleeing unemployment, unrest, and a dearth of options, have settled uneasily and awkwardly into *gecekondu* ("built overnight") neighborhoods in what were once the far outskirts of a medium-sized city. Istanbul, not Diyarbakır in the southeast, has Turkey's largest Kurdish population. According to Turkey's national statistics institute, nearly one-third of urban Turks live in a *gecekondu*. These are not slums, but more like transplanted villages. There is a feel of community about them, and they are fertile fields for the conservative and Islamic political parties.

Other, non-Turkish population groups are also on the rise. After the breakup of the USSR, economic refugees from former Soviet republics flooded into Istanbul. Some are doing big business and there is a lot of talk about a Russian "mafia," but often the immigrants are trying to eke out a living selling anything from shoddy alarm clocks to themselves (the Turkish slang for prostitute is "Natasha"). As Turkey moves closer to the European Union, more investment is coming from EU countries and, with it, more European companies and business executives.

For Ben and me, this all seems fascinating. The city is increasingly cosmopolitan and beginning to have as rich a mix of nationalities as Ottoman Istanbul.

Our neighbors didn't deny it when we pointed out that old-time Istanbul families sometimes see only the erosion of the smaller, simpler Istanbul they grew up with. They cluck at the rough ways of the Anatolian peasants, resent the newcomers and their need for space. They sneer at the swagger of the Mercedes- or SUV-driving nouveaux riches and yearn for what they remember as more elegant times. The movement of villagers to the city has brought a new conservatism and religious consciousness that is not welcomed by the secular elite. *Istanbullu*s begin to blame any and all urban ills on the newcomers.

Traditional Turkish hospitality and civility survive, though the overcrowding and traffic take their toll on *Istanbullu* nerves. *Trafik canavarı* ("traffic monster," the Turkish equivalent of "road rage") has entered the vocabulary. New buildings of questionable architectural taste pop up where gentle green spaces and orchards used to be, and new roads to accommodate the traffic are thrown up in front of formerly waterside villas.

Urban sprawl has created an Istanbul larger in area than the state of Rhode Island and larger in population than Belgium or Greece.

Every day more "internal immigrants" leave their villages to try their luck in Istanbul; every day hundreds of additional cars move into the already paralyzed traffic.

Mike interrupted: "What about the economy? Are all these people finding jobs? I thought Turkey was supposed to be a poor country, but I see a lot of signs of wealth."

One of our neighbors winced. We remembered that after the economic downturn in early 2001, he told us that he had lost half his wealth. The lira lost half its value overnight, and all his holdings were in liras, not dollars or other foreign currency. With the economic crisis of 2001, unemployment and underemployment skyrocketed, and many an affluent *Istanbullu* had to rethink spending habits.

Even so, Istanbul remains resilient and vibrant, and the recession seems to be lifting. After years of runaway inflation, the Turkish lira is holding fairly steady, and, in 2005, for the first time in years, the dollar actually lost value against the lira.

After a moment, our neighbor suppressed his thoughts about his own financial troubles and said, "Getting a firm grip on the state of Istanbul's economy is not easy. Turkey, like Italy, has a 'black' economy at least as large as the official one. Is this a 'poor' city or a 'wealthy' one? It's hard to say. Yes, there is a lot of wealth in this city. No matter how bad the economic crisis, the restaurants are always crowded, the Mercedes dealers continue to find customers. There isn't an easy answer. Istanbul's streets are full of rich and poor, young and old, urban and rural, Eastern and Western, old *Istanbullu* and newcomer. Some residents struggle to make ends meet, but others spend at a breathtaking pace. It is possible to buy a single cigarette from a street vendor, but I can also show you fantastic restaurants where you can order the finest French champagne."

He's right. Istanbul's contrasts can be startling, charming, even unsettling—but Istanbul is never dull.

"How about cultural life?" Mike asked. In fact, he had timed his visit to coincide with the Istanbul International Music Festival. Through our fellow islander and good friend, Nilgün, an official with the festivals, we were able to get tickets for their outstanding

Turkish and international programs during Mike's stay.

I jumped in at this point. "That's one of the reasons we moved here," I reminded Mike. "This is my kind of place: a city teeming with cultural life. And here you get the best of both East and West. You can find anything from traditional Turkish folk music to avant-garde installation art. The international festivals draw top artists from around the world and use venues ranging from simple theaters to magnificent sites like Haghia Sophia and Topkapı Palace. State-subsidized opera, ballet, and symphony presentations are priced low enough for nearly anyone to afford a ticket. Dozens of private venues offer music, dance, theater, and film. Turkish artists have walked away with top European awards, including the jury prize at the Cannes film festival and the Eurovision music competition first prize. For architecture buffs, the historic buildings alone could fill a lifetime of study and travel. It would be impossible to take it all in."

But the nostalgia of the longtime *Istanbullu* surfaced.

"Maybe so," said our neighbor, "but Istanbul isn't what it used to be. In the 1970s and even early 1980s, what a beautiful city this was. Ah, if only you'd known it *then*."

This was punctuated by a heavy sigh. It's a common refrain, but then along comes a new visitor or new resident, seeing Istanbul for the first time and falling in love with it just as others have throughout the ages. They see that with all its growing pains, Istanbul is still a magnificent city. Its hills, noble skyline, sweeping sea vistas, grand monuments, its plethora of sounds and colors and aromas—and especially the traditional *Istanbullu* grace and hospitality—still work their magic on those prepared to receive and appreciate what Istanbul can offer.

******

Now we were ready to plan Mike's tour. He would do the usual, entry-level tourist circuit on his own—the old city, including Sultanahmet, the Grand Bazaar, the Spice Market, and Kariye Museum; on the other side of the Golden Horn, Dolmabahçe Palace, Rümeli Hisarı, and a boat trip up the Bosphorus.

For our look at "real" Istanbul, there were a lot of choices.

Istanbul has always been a city of defined neighborhoods and districts, many of which retain their special character even now in these days of greater mobility. At one time, specific areas of the city even had characteristic dialects. A few words from an *Istanbullu* would have allowed a Turkish Henry Higgins to identify exactly where the speaker was raised. That has largely disappeared, but the neighborhoods remain individual enough to offer a variety of experiences. Istanbul lifestyles range from terminally hip to deeply traditional.

We discussed several options and wanted to make this a one-day tour to show that the contrasts still lie close together in this megalopolis. One of the most appealing things about Istanbul is the way all these possibilities intersect. Ben and I checked the boat schedules and other transportation options, and settled on a plan. A day spent in Eyüp, Kadıköy, and Beyoğlu would give Mike a good sampling.

Traditional Istanbul

Istanbul's most traditional, conservative neighborhoods are, appropriately enough, in the old city, particularly along the Golden Horn. For that side of Istanbul, we could have taken Mike to Fatih, a fiercely conservative district named for the mosque of Fatih Sultan Mehmet (Mehmet the Conqueror). It has long been a neighborhood apart. In his 1879 novel *Aziyadé*, French writer Pierre Loti said of Fatih: "This is the center of completely oriental activity: camels move through it at their quiet pace…; dervishes come to sit and speak at leisure about holy things, and nothing has yet arrived from the West." The camels are long gone and the West now shows its face in Fatih, but the neighborhood remains a symbol of the Islamic side of Turkish life.

For Mike, though, we decided on a visit to Eyüp, a village at the end of the Golden Horn. We took an early ferry from Heybeliada, disembarking at the end of the line, Sirkeci. From there, it's a ten-minute walk along the Golden Horn, under the bridge, and on to a small pier at Eminönü with hourly motor launches up the Golden

Horn.

We had a few minutes before the next boat to Eyüp, so we strolled on the paths alongside the Golden Horn, giving Mike a few photo ops and adjusting ourselves to the traffic noise of the city.

The half-hour boat trip to Eyüp from Eminönü is a pleasant one, with stops at Balat, an old Jewish quarter now undergoing renovation with funding from UNESCO, and Fener, the site of the Greek Orthodox Patriarchate. Eyüp is the end of the line. Stepping off the boat and into the crowded village seems like travel back in time.

The mosque at Eyüp, the burial place of Mohammed's standard bearer Eyüp Ensari, is one of Islam's holiest pilgrimage sites and draws huge numbers of visitors, both Turkish and foreign. The milling crowds, the street merchants offering food and souvenirs, the sense of being in a sacred place: all these create something of what must have been the atmosphere of medieval cathedrals on pilgrimage days. Like France's Reims Cathedral, the Eyüp mosque complex was doubly important as a major religious shrine and as the site of royal "coronations" (in the Ottoman world, the sultan was not crowned but girded with the sword of Osman, founder of the Ottoman dynasty).

As we began our stroll around the narrow streets, the 21st century intruded again in the form of cars, trucks, and blaring music. We bought some *simit*s to eat as we headed into some of the smaller, quieter streets.

The Eyüp district was at one time a favorite countryside escape for Istanbul residents, the site of royal palaces and pavilions. It was a picturesque place with romantic vistas and known for "the sweet waters of Europe," two small streams that flowed into the Golden Horn. By the late 20th century, pollution and industrial "progress" had spoiled some of the earlier beauty, but recent municipal efforts have made significant improvements and restored some of Eyüp's former charm. For Westerners, particularly the French, Eyüp is best known as one of the settings for Pierre Loti's *Aziyadé*. His memory lives on in a small café bearing his name. It is not the café that Loti frequented, but is a pleasant place to while away an afternoon.

We wanted Mike to see Eyüp as an excursion into an older Istanbul with a very different worldview and pace from that of the rest of the city. It is not a place for a quick visit or a set itinerary. This is a place for strolling, wandering, and following the flow of humanity that has come here out of Islamic piety and/or interest in Istanbul's Ottoman past.

As we munched on our *simit*s, we took our time, admiring the greenery, listening to the songs of the birds and the conversations of the pilgrims. We stopped to look at religious and non-religious goods being offered by street merchants, including brochures on how to live a holy life. We translated some of the titles for Mike, and he decided he had to have one called "100 Duties of a Good Wife." We stepped aside as he and the merchant bargained enthusiastically without a common language.

We joined the line for entry to the mosque and tomb of Eyüp, removing our shoes at the door and following the crowds past the exquisite Iznik tiles and waiting in another line to view the footprint of the prophet Mohammed. As we exited the building and retrieved our shoes, we sat for a few minutes to observe the other visitors.

Mike perked up and reached for his camera when he saw a family group approaching, all of them fussing over a young boy. He was wearing a glittering white suit and cape with gold piping, bow tie, feathered hat, and a sash with gold lettering spelling out *Maşallah!* ("May God protect him!") In his hand was a gold staff with ornate orb. Then Mike spotted another similarly dressed boy…and another.

"What's going on?" he asked.

"Must be circumcision season," we replied matter-of-factly.

"Excuse me? Circumcision *season*?"

Maybe we've been here too long to realize what sounds strange to foreigners.

"Sorry. Yes. Turkish boys are circumcised after the age of five, but before they get to their teens. It's a rite of passage, more or less like a Bar mitzvah or Confirmation, with a big party after the deed is done. Many of them come here before the operation as an act of piety. The boys get a lot of presents and attention, but we always wonder if they fully realize what's about to happen. It is considered very shameful for a boy to cry or carry on; if he does, the family will never let him forget."

These boys were obviously in the pre-operation mode, having a great time, feeling quite proud of themselves in their special costumes, and patiently posing for endless photos. We reminded Mike to ask before taking pictures of the boys or their families, but all were more than happy to oblige.

We then decided to visit the old cemetery with its evocative atmosphere and fascinating tombstones (shaped like turbans for men and flowers for women). Finally, we settled into the Pierre Loti café for tea and one of the best views in Istanbul. Eighty years of secularism have made Turkey a modern, Western country, but a visit to Eyüp is a reminder of the country's Islamic roots and the continuing fervor of its believers.

Mike's camera got a good workout in Eyüp, but it was time to catch the boat back to Eminönü, where we could take a ferry from another of the piers and head for Kadıköy.

Blending Old and New

For shopping, tourists can find everything they need at Istanbul's famous and picturesque Grand Bazaar. The affluent *Istanbullu* has high-end contemporary shopping districts. On the European side, there is Akmerkez, one of the world's priciest shopping malls, offering everything from Rolex watches to Armani suits, from Godiva chocolate to the latest electronics. Another upscale district is the Asian side's main boulevard, Bağdat Caddesi (Baghdad Avenue, following the route of an old road from Istanbul to Baghdad). This is Istanbul's Rodeo Drive, lined with wide sidewalks, designer fashion, restaurants, cafes, pastry shops, high-end home décor shops, electronics suppliers, offices, and more. It has no special appeal for the tourist—there are few, if any, shops selling traditional crafts nor are there many buildings of historical interest along the street. But it's where the modern *Istanbullu* goes to shop, see, and be seen. It is always clogged with traffic, and hundreds if not thousands of young, chic *Istanbullu*s stroll along the avenue at all hours. A headscarf or other "Islamic" dress is a rare sight. When Starbucks finally decided to try out the Turkish market, its first shops were inside Akmerkez and on Bağdat Caddesi.

Those two shopping options are great if we need a shot of U.S.-style affluence and consumerism, but we seldom go there. My favorite shopping district is on the Asian side of Istanbul, in Kadıköy, at the northern end of Bağdat Caddesi. That's where we were now taking Mike. The district combines history, tradition, and 21st-century progress. It is a place not only to shop, but also to study Istanbul's past, present, and future.

On the ferry we gave Mike the historical background: Kadıköy, formerly Chalcedon, was the earliest settlement in what is now Istanbul. Established in the 7th century B.C. by Megarians fleeing Greece, today's Kadıköy was ruled, over the centuries, by Persians, Greeks, Bithynians, Romans, Byzantines, and Ottomans. Another Megarian, Byzas, founder of Byzantium, had been told by the Oracle of Delphi to establish his city "opposite the land of the blind." When Byzas saw the strategically perfect hill above the Golden Horn (where Topkapı Palace stands today), he understood that you would have to be "blind" to have settled on the opposite shore as the founders of Chalcedon had done. Byzas' choice became the center of the Byzantine Empire and passed to the Ottomans when they conquered Istanbul in 1453.

Kadıköy's history was not as glorious as that of its neighbor across the water, and by the late 20th century, the few sites of historical interest had either disappeared or become dwarfed by the new construction in the area. As Istanbul underwent rapid urban expansion, this became a densely populated district and a major commercial center.

It's a short ferry ride from Eminönü to Kadıköy, but Mike got a chance for close-up shots of Haydarpaşa railway terminal and distance shots of Topkapı Palace and the Galata Tower. As we left the ferry, we took our time making our way through the crowd. We investigated the stalls offering fresh flowers and potted plants, live birds and fish. At the open square nearby, people were setting up booths and lighting for a Black Sea festival scheduled for that evening; one of them handed us a flyer and encouraged us to come back to eat and dance all evening. We continued on, ignoring the gypsy women selling flowers and the lineup of men at their ornate brass shoeshine stands.

Crossing the main street, we soon plunged into the market district. The shopping in Kadıköy has something for everyone. The covered area has the charm of the *Kapalı Çarşı* (Grand Bazaar) and the food shops are as tempting as the ones in the *Mısır Çarşısı* (Spice Market), but without the touristic overlays. There is an antiques district and a good choice of cafes and restaurants for the weary shopper.

We went first to the food market. Though Istanbul has plenty of large, conventional supermarkets, I prefer Kadıköy's more colorful traditional market with individual merchants competing for customers, their goods spilling out from their inside showcases to eye-catching, outdoor displays. Glistening greens and fragrant seasonal fruits beckoned from a corner *manav* (greengrocer); seductive aromas wafted from an "artisanal" bakery; the deep colors—magenta and saffron and crimson—of spices piled high in street-side bins made their way into Mike's lens; and I checked to be sure that the fishmonger still had his pet goose. One specialty shop offers only olives and olive products; another features comb honey and homemade jams so fresh they are still warm. Mundane grocery shopping becomes an aesthetic pleasure in Kadıköy, far from the confines of a shopping cart and aisles. Mike snapped his photos happily while Ben and I stocked up on a few things we can't find on the island.

We continued along the narrow streets to the antiques market, which still has prices far lower than those at the more famous Hor Hor or Çukurcuma antiques centers on the European side of Istanbul. We stopped for a few minutes to watch one of the last of the old-style coppersmiths, still hammering out decorative copper trays by hand. Not far away is another shopping area with passageways devoted to bookstores, computer shops, and some of Istanbul's ubiquitous cell phone suppliers. It has become a main haunt of Istanbul's intellectuals.

We didn't take Mike to another Kadıköy landmark: a recent (2003) shopping mall with a huge supermarket; high-end shops offering household goods, electronics, and jewelry; and a (to me) nightmare food court with nothing Turkish at all...only American fast food. Shopping malls like this one have proliferated on the outskirts of Turkey's major cities, but this is the first such place in the city center. So far, it seems to be doing only moderate business. Some welcome it for its convenience, but others revile it as out of place in this part of Istanbul. We've been there a couple of times for hard-to-find computer items.

Kadıköy is always crowded, always lively, and each visit reveals something we hadn't seen or noticed before. One time we stumbled on Istanbul's largest and grandest old movie theater, originally built by an Ottoman pasha as his personal opera house. That day with Mike, we finally noticed and went inside the Armenian church in the heart of the market. Nearby, in the Moda neighborhood, we once visited a tiny British church, legacy of a former British enclave in the area. Kadıköy offers shopping, food, and history, but best of all, unlike Sultanahmet, it is free of tour buses and of touts trying to lure foreigners into their shops. We had a quick bite to eat at one of the kebab stands and prepared for the *pièce de résistance*: Beyoğlu.

Contemporary Istanbul

By now Mike had been given a full dose of Islamic Istanbul in Eyüp, and a look at the blend of old and new in a middle-class neighborhood, Kadıköy. Now it was time to show him the vibrant heart of Istanbul: Taksim Square and Istiklal.

From Kadıköy we took a ferry to Karaköy, at the northern side of the Galata Bridge on the Golden Horn. From there, we rode the Tünel, Europe's third-oldest, shortest, and certainly most charming subway. Its two cars, one starting from each end, are the same model as older Paris Métro cars and have the same distinctive tone as the doors close. There is only one stop, with the entire journey taking ninety seconds. After this brief moment in France, we were at the top of the hill, at the foot of Istiklal Caddesi (Independence Avenue), known in Ottoman times as the "Grande Rue de Pera," the heart of non-Muslim Istanbul.

Running from the Tünel to Taksim Square, Istiklal today is a pedestrian street, about two kilometers long, lined with restaurants, cafes, bookshops, art galleries, cinemas, clothing stores, music stores, and dozens of intriguing passageways and lanes leading to small shops and nightclubs. We pointed out the old-fashioned tram that runs up the middle of Istiklal, clanging at pedestrians to move aside, but recommended to Mike that we walk. Istiklal is an outdoor museum of Art Nouveau architecture, one of the best-preserved collections in the world, and the former embassies in this area now house some of the world's most elegant consulates.

Mike was skeptical at first. He saw no reason to look at this more Western face of Istanbul. That wasn't what he came to Turkey to see. But Istiklal can seduce anyone. Whether you're looking for antiques or jazz clubs, a mosque or a Burger King, funky Indian shirts or designer clothes, simplicity or elegance, you'll find it here.

As we exited the Tünel, there were already too many choices. We could turn down Galip Dede Caddesi and stroll past the musical instrument ateliers, music stores, and whirling dervish center near the Galata Tower. Or we could head immediately in the other direction, up Istiklal, into Istanbul's most vibrant neighborhood, with its mix of artists, writers, journalists, foreigners, and musicians. There are art galleries, restaurants, coffee houses, jazz clubs, and cultural centers along with shops and consulates. In fact, the two areas are rapidly blending into one irresistible paradise for young Turks and foreigners.

Ben and I puzzled over it for a moment. Across from the Tünel we could browse through antique prints and postcards...or a few paces farther along, we could enter a beautifully restored, now trendy arcade leading to Sofyalı Sokak's art galleries and restaurants. Or we could take a detour to see the Pera Palas Hotel, where Agatha Christie, Mata Hari, Greta Garbo and many other celebrities have stayed Or we could visit the dervish museum.

No, we decided to go straight up Istiklal, past the Swedish consulate in its beautiful garden, stopping first at Markiz Patisserie. Closed for decades, Markiz was reopened in 2004 after being restored to its full Art Nouveau splendor. It has re-emerged as one of the finest examples among Istanbul's rich heritage of *Belle Époque* buildings.

As we continued along Istiklal, Mike listened more closely to the music coming from the myriad music shops along the avenue; he inhaled the aromas from restaurants, cafes, perfume dealers, and spice shops. He marveled at the former embassies, now used as consulates, and at the new home of the Greek consulate in a beautifully renovated building. He was surprised at the number of English-language offerings in a large bookstore that stocks only books, maps, and CDs about Istanbul.

Mike checked out the fashions in the display windows and on the crowds of young *Istanbullu*s along the street. On a side street we stopped at a small shop selling one-of-a-kind creations crafted from cloth imported from Uzbekistan. On Istiklal, he found easy-to-pack gifts at Ipek, a friendly shop selling elegant silk scarves with Ottoman designs and low price tags. Harder to pack were the recreations of Ottoman-era glassware from Paşabahçe, the outlet for the famous glass factory on the Asian side of Istanbul.

We watched a wedding party going into one of Istiklal's 19th century churches. These Catholic and Protestant churches are still well attended, and some offer concerts from time to time. We examined the junky merchandise on small street carts and Mike took photos of some of Istiklal's ever-present street characters: a *köfte* (meatball) seller dressed in a pharmacist's white coat, standing ramrod straight and expressionless; a small man with exaggerated mutton chop whiskers, a Tyrolean hat, giant worry beads, and apparently nothing to sell; gypsy women selling small bunches of lavender. Ben watched for a particular outdoor news kiosk; its sweet-faced young owner in headscarf somehow manages to get the new edition of *The Economist* before anyone else in town.

We had already eaten in Kadıköy, but pointed out some of the famous restaurants along the way: Rejans, established by refugee White Russians shortly after the Bolshevik revolution and frequented by Atatürk in the 1920s and '30s; Haci Baba, Haci Abdullah, or Haci Salih, all masters of traditional Turkish cuisine; the Nevizade Street *meyhane*s behind the overly gentrified Çiçek Pasajı near the imposing Galatasaray High School. "If we decide to stay into the evening," we said to Mike, "we can have dinner at Saki. The owners of that *meyhane* used to be waiters at other restaurants, but decided to go into business for themselves. The food is great."

In the meantime, we gave Mike a few options. He preferred to keep wandering off the main avenue into some of the small shop-lined "passages" and down the hill to the "French Street," a replica of a Paris neighborhood in the heart of Istanbul. We could see that he was getting caught up in the energy and vitality of Istiklal Caddesi. Within a few minutes this jaded New Yorker couldn't stop saying, "This is so hip. I had no idea. How long can we stay?" We had covered only half the length of the street and were still far from Taksim Square. There was a lot to see in between.

"No problem," we said. "Let's take our time. You may not be back here again." We had planned on catching the early evening commuter boat from Kabataş, just down the hill from Taksim Square. In fact, we had to rush to catch the very last boat back to Heybeliada from Sirkeci late that night. When we got back to the island house and settled in with a *rakı* nightcap, Mike was already making plans for next year's return visit.

XVII
LION'S MILK

The best accompaniment to *rakı* is good conversation.
Mustafa Kemal Atatürk

A word of explanation. Turkey is known for two milky white drinks. One is *ayran,* a refreshing yogurt drink similar to buttermilk. The other—and by far the more interesting of the two—is *rakı,* affectionately known to Turks as *aslan sütü,* "lion's milk." Ayran is fine with lunch, but our island evenings usually include generous lashings of *rakı.*

Rakı is the national drink, but not the island's only option. The national liquor monopoly, Tekel, produces whisky, gin, vodka, rum, cognac, and several liqueurs—none of them much good. There is excellent beer that is, to my taste, far better than watery American beers. Wine in Turkey has a distinguished history: the cultivation of grapes for wine began in Anatolia more than 6,000 years ago, and archeologists have found evidence of a very early vineyard near Mt. Ararat, where Noah's Ark is said to have landed. In more modern times, Tekel has been a major wine producer, but Turkish wine connoisseurs pay far more attention to the increasingly sophisticated, and expensive, wines from private firms.

Wine and beer consumption are important in Turkey, but there is no question about the national drink. Turkey would not be Turkey without *rakı,* the anise-flavored drink that serves as aperitif, meal enhancer, and digestif all in one. There are anise-flavored drinks throughout the Mediterranean region: *ouzo* in Greece, *arak* in the Arab world, and the more distant relative, French *pastis.* But *rakı* has a unique taste and style. No one would drink *pastis* with a meal, but many Turks consider *rakı* the only possible choice with a tray of *meze.*

Many foreigners don't like *rakı.* That's fine with Turks. Many Turkish women drink *rakı;* many more do not. But a Turkish man who doesn't drink *rakı* is a rarity, maybe even a little bit suspect (can he really be a Turk?). Kadri is the only one of our island friends who never touches the stuff.

In restaurants on Heybeliada, as elsewhere in Turkey, the *rakı* arrives first, before the meal begins, setting off a flurry of activity assembling the needed glasses, water, and ice. In the bottle, *rakı* is as clear as vodka, but, when water is added, it turns a pale white, the color of skim milk. No matter how many times we saw this magical transformation in restaurants, at friend's houses, in our own garden, it remained puzzling. *Rakı* is not pure alcohol; it contains plenty of water. So, why, then, does the addition of more water make it turn white?

Ben and I couldn't figure it out. We had many opportunities to ask around. We know a lot of dedicated Heybeliada *rakıcılar* (*rakı* aficionados), but no one had an answer. No one had ever stopped to wonder. We began reading whatever we could find about the drink. Turkey's *Gusto* magazine, "dedicated to the culture of drink," had a special issue on *rakı* with information on its ingredients, on its manufacture, on its history, but nothing to explain the mystery. Finally, it was an American visitor to Heybeliada, tasting his first *rakı*, who provided the simple answer. Apparently, not one of our island *rakıcılar* is a scientist. Our visiting American, a chemist named David, reluctantly put down his glass of *rakı* for a moment and formed his thumbs and forefingers into a triangle.

"Look," he said, "let's call this triangle a diagram of *rakı* as it comes in the bottle. There are three elements: the alcohol, the water, and the flavoring oils (the anise flavor). All are in perfect suspension, so the liquid remains clear."

OK, that makes sense so far.

"When you add more water," David said as he lifted one forefinger, "that balance is destroyed and the oils blend with the alcohol and water, turning the *rakı* white."

Well, he probably explained it a little more carefully and scientifically, but that's the best rendition I can give. After all, we'd all had a couple of rounds before the question came up. In any case, it all became clear. And I remembered David's words some weeks later when the waiters at an outdoor restaurant in old Stamboul were amusing themselves and their customers by carefully layering water and *rakı* in a glass, forming a sort of Turkish pousse-café. They somehow managed to keep the balance steady while they poured. Many a *rakıcı* would disapprove of this parlor trick. *Rakı*, like soccer, is not to be trifled with.

Most *rakı* aficionados love the ceremony of preparing a glass just the way they like it. Our island *rakıcılar* can argue for hours about the "right" way to drink lion's milk. A few drink it neat, with a glass of water as a chaser. Most mix the *rakı* with water, but not all add ice. There is great controversy over whether the ice or the water should be added first. But the greatest arguments are over which *rakı* is best.

All over the world, drinkers have a fondness for ranking their tipples and finding ways to judge other drinkers as cognoscenti or mere amateurs. Wine tasting events are one example. The need for bartenders to ask which vodka or gin should go in the martini is another. Single-malt whiskies have their loyal followings. But in Turkey, all *rakı* came from the same manufacturer: the government monopoly, Tekel. To introduce some variety, they created a few different brands, but the largest selling *rakı* was always Yeni ("new"), the drink of the average *rakıcı*.

The process of producing *rakı* is fairly simple. It is basically grape alcohol with fragrant aniseed oil added after the initial fermentation. Tekel officials insist that there is no difference in the proportions of alcohol and aniseed from factory to factory. *Rakı*, they insist, is *rakı*.

But if everyone is drinking the same *rakı*, how can they separate the "real" *rakıcılar* from the amateurs? Another system of ranking developed. Although Tekel produces all bottles of Yeni *rakı*, there are several factories around the country. A mythology developed that the best Yeni *rakı* came from the factory in Tekirdağ, an otherwise unremarkable town on the road from Istanbul to Gallipoli. Why Tekirdağ? "It's the water," the *rakıcılar* would reply, echoing old

American beer ads. They would examine bottles carefully to check the codes on the caps. Certain combinations of letters and numbers were "known" to indicate the factory of origin, but these codes varied, depending on the person doing the deciphering. And it was later revealed that the Tekel directors changed the codes from time to time. In any case, it made for wonderful restaurant theater as indignant *rakıcılar* sent back bottles with the "wrong" codes.

Government monopolies usually have little flair for advertising, but a brilliant scheme was unveiled just after the turn of the millennium. A new *rakı* with an advanced price and a distinctive bottle shape appeared on the market. Its brand name is Tekirdağ and every bottle is guaranteed to be from the legendary factory. Island grocers' shelves began to fill with bottles of Tekirdağ and it became de rigueur to offer the new brand whenever a host wanted to impress his guests. But it took some of the fun out of *rakı* drinking for those who love a good argument. Island restaurants seemed a bit quieter.

Just when I had nearly given up on the chances for theatrical *rakı* arguments, a new, private-sector *rakı* appeared on the market. Another soon followed, this one named for one of the Princes' Islands. At that point, some of the stalwart Heybeli *rakıcılar* began to admit that they didn't really like Tekirdağ's sweeter, stronger taste. Others said they were crazy. Aficionados starting lining up behind their favorites. Voices rose.

The floodgates had opened. More new private-sector *rakı* brands have hit the market. There were some three dozen brands at last count and there is no end in sight. A random sampling indicates that they are definitely not all the same. Some are sweeter, some are stronger, some are no good at all. Dim the lights. The drama has resumed. I am already hearing firm declarations and arguments in favor of this one or that one. Maybe one of them will even make a convert of Kadri.

XVIII
WEEKLY MARKET

You don't have to cook fancy or complicated masterpieces—just good food from
fresh ingredients.
>
> Julia Child

The red-roofed Heybeliada houses cascade down the eastern
slope of Değirmen Hill, facing north or northeast across the Sea of
Marmara. There is a practical reason for this: islanders' desire to
avoid the harsh *lodos* winds from the south and southwest. But as an
unplanned bonus, this placement provides one of the most satisfying
island moments.

Sitting on the front balcony at dawn, we can watch the beautiful
colors in the morning sky as the sun rises over the Asian shore of
Istanbul. At that hour, even the stray cats are not yet stirring, and it
will be another hour before the *fayton* drivers fetch their horses from
the stables near the pine forest. At dawn, the only sound is the ever-
present cry of seagulls. Some days that beautiful silence can extend
until 7:30 or 8:00 a.m., broken only by the occasional footsteps of
someone hurrying down the hill to catch the first ferry into Istanbul.

Not on Wednesdays. That is market day. Municipal workers and
private entrepreneurs start early to prepare the tables, tarps, and stall
assignments well before the first farmers arrive with their goods.
Nearly all the merchants come from the agricultural area near
Yalova, across the Sea of Marmara, bringing their produce, cheeses,
or housewares to Heybeliada by ferry or on smaller, chartered boats.
I love to walk down to the water's edge on Wednesday mornings to
watch the market activity.

The first ferry from Yalova arrives at 7:00 a.m., carrying mostly
small-time sellers with pushcarts or just a basketful of items to sell.
Ferry officials try to collect the excess-baggage chits from exiting
merchants, who are preoccupied with getting their goods safely and
quickly on shore. Meanwhile, island commuters jostle their way

onto the ferry before it continues on to central Istanbul.

As the merchants make their way from the ferry to the market area, I observe what they're bringing. A prosperous-looking man smiles proudly to himself as he sees me admiring the cheeses and olives on his cart. An old woman in headscarf and overcoat is clutching her paltry goods: a few packages of paper napkins, tea strainers, odds and ends. The profit on these hardly seems enough to pay for her boat fare. Some carry odd combinations of goods to sell: paper towels and cucumbers, clothespins and spices.

At the commercial dock down the way, at the foot of the main market street, the first of the chartered boats has arrived. There is only one at this early hour, but as the morning progresses, there will be eight or nine at a time, jockeying for docking space, each loaded with dozens of crates and flats of fruits, vegetables, eggs, and other goods. As the farmers get their wares onto the dock, they transfer them to waiting carts and wagons in every conceivable shape and size, some as simple as a cardboard box lashed to a dolly. No horses are used here, just human labor. There is enough unemployment or underemployment to ensure a supply of men, young and old, to move the goods up the slope to the market. In the early hours, while the market area is still fairly empty, the youngest of them relieve the drudgery by careering back down the hill using the empty crates as toboggans.

City officials handle the rental of stalls at the market, which spreads out over several residential streets. The most expensive spaces are on the main market street stretching up from the dock; the cheapest, at the far edges of the market area. There is no argument about where to place the goods. Each merchant has a specific spot. A private entrepreneur supplies crude wooden tables, with reduced rates for rental of four or more. Some of the smallest merchants simply pile up their own crates and work from those.

Already, at 7:00 a.m., merchants are staking out their places and arranging their tables. Some stretch canopies—protection against either sun or rain—across the road, and tie the ropes to anything handy: fences, trees, or shrubs in front of neighbors' houses. The market won't be in full operation until at least 9:00 a.m., so the farmers take time to be sure their displays are just right. Meanwhile, I drop by one of the cafes to sip tea until the market is ready to begin.

Wherever I am in the world, I always seek out a farmers' market. They, like the language, tell a lot about the culture. In San Francisco, the Ferry Building's farmers' market is a gourmet destination prized by the most discriminating foodies. In Brussels, I learned that it is impossible to ask for a kilo of potatoes. There are at least a dozen varieties and you need to know which is needed for the dish you want to make. At the Heybeli market, I soon learned the distinction between vegetables to be served cold with olive oil (*zeytinyağlı*) and those to be cooked with meat and served hot (*etli*). The variety of green bean you buy depends on whether it is going to be *zeytinyağlı* or *etli*.

Turkish greengrocers have a gift for artistic display and a keen sense of how to tempt customers' eyes, noses, and taste buds. They arrange their goods with as much intensity as any artist at an easel. Some of the best examples are pushed forward, with the "seconds" saved in back for end-of-day sales or for unpleasant customers. The best of the best will also be held back for regular customers. To trump competitors selling similar foods, some merchants will offer hesitating customers a convincing taste.

One of the kings of the market is the melon man, Yaşar, who rents one of the best spots. He creates a decorative backdrop, puts down a bedding of straw and greenery to highlight his melons, and splits open one of each variety to show the luscious colors. It creates the effect of a nomadic tent waiting to offer refreshment to the passerby.

The Heybeliada market is strictly seasonal and mostly local. Or if not from Yalova, the produce is at least from somewhere in Turkey. The weekly array of dried fruits and nuts brings plump, sweet dried apricots from Malatya, a southeastern city known for its apricots and its politicians (two of Turkey's ten presidents were from Malatya).

Each week's market is slightly different, changing with the season. Island shoppers know when each fruit or vegetable will be at its peak, and they converge on the stands offering the week's best produce. I soon learned to watch carefully and move fast. If I am lucky enough to spot the Mavi Restaurant owner doing her shopping, I note what passes muster with her. If it meets her high standards, whatever it is, I'll buy some, too.

As a Californian, I never understood the East Coast fondness for changing seasons, but, now, watching the seasonal changes at the Heybeliada market has opened my eyes to the advantages. In May, there is a fleeting chance to buy fresh rose petals, heaped in straw baskets and ready to be made into rose jam. The sweet strawberries of May give way to the enormous Napoleon cherries in June (but why "Napoleon" for the largest size?). As the cherries begin to fade into memory, fresh apricots take the stage until the peaches—possibly Turkey's most luscious fruit—begin to make their appearance, reaching their peak in August. Because Turkey has many climates and growing areas, some fruits reappear as the season ends in one region and begins in another. As summer draws to a close, we begin to find wonderful figs of many sizes and colors and the first of the succulent grapes and numerous varieties of pears ranging from pale green to deep purple. And so on through the seasons.

Some of these offerings have fanciful names. "Napoleon" cherries are one example, though one of our neighbors gets confused and asks for "Bonaparte." There used to be "Washington" apples—not from the American northwest, but the best quality from Turkey. I asked why they were called "Washington." In the 1950s, when Turkey had just joined NATO, and Turkish soldiers were fighting alongside American troops in Korea, it was the golden age of U.S.-Turkish relations. "Washington" became an adjective to describe something superlative. The usage stuck for apples. During the same period, "Russian salad," the familiar potato and pea salad in mayonnaise, became known in Turkey as "American salad" and is still called by that name.

I usually try to do my market shopping by 10:00 a.m. After that, the market is full. By 11:30 there is barely room to maneuver. Thrifty housewives wait until the afternoon when the farmers drop their prices to rock bottom to avoid carrying their goods back onto the boats to Yalova. But I sometimes get discounts, too, by coming early. Mine can often be the first sale of the day (*şifta*) and receive a lower price from a merchant whose superstitions see this as the first sign of a successful day, passing the money across his face for good luck.

By now I am well into the market, dodging the two-wheeled shopping carts that nearly everyone brings. For those who don't, there are boys and men waiting with oversized baskets—or, more often, a large cardboard box on wheels—to follow the shopper around and deliver the purchases home for a minuscule fee. When they hear how far up the hill I want them to take things, though, they either move on or quote an absurdly high price. Their cries mingle with those of the merchants:

"Empty cart available."

"Gorgeous figs over here"

"Perfect onions for your fish"

"*Abla,* look at my spices!"

"You must need pine nuts. Don't you ever make *dolma*s?"

"Empty cart. Service direct to your house."

"Try these beans. They're as sweet as sugar."

The melon king, Yaşar, always ready to outdo everyone else, sings his message, fitting the words into traditional Turkish melodies. In spring, he sings "Adana Ceyhan" to announce that his early season melons are not only from Adana (the best), but from the Ceyhan region of Adana (best of the best). The "lyrics" change as other regions' melons come into season.

Making a success of the stall next to Yaşar is a challenge, but the neighboring fruit seller, Şakir, competes by catching the shopper's eye, not ear. In late May, he places mounds of cherries around his stand, puts an eye-catching early-season apricot atop each "hill," and finishes it with a branch of cherry leaves placed in the center. "Where's your camera?" Şakir calls. "Take a photo of my cherry orchard."

At Turkish markets, cheese, eggs, olives, and *yufka* (the wide, thin circles of dough similar to Greek *phyllo)* are usually sold at the same stand. The olives, several varieties both green and black, are in large tubs and make a handsome contrast to the all-white cheese, eggs, and *yufka*. At the market, as in most Turkish grocery shops, eggs are sold individually, not in cartons or dozens. Each size is a different price. Among the four competing merchants of cheese, eggs, olives, and *yufka* at the Heybeli market, my loyalty went immediately to one of them because of the eggs.

"How many eggs, *abla*?" he asked.

"Ten, please," I replied as I watched him grab a few from each pile. "Why are you picking some from each group?"

"They're all different prices. I don't like to make change. This way your total comes to an even number."

Makes sense to me, so I'm willing to ask first for whatever cheese or olives I need, leaving the eggs for last so he can top off his calculations. Sometimes he'll even suggest that I adjust the number of eggs to help him come out at an even lira amount.

Turkey has an abundance of milk from cows, goats and sheep, but the varieties of cheese are fairly limited. The main offerings are *beyaz peynir* ("white cheese," the Turkish feta*), kaşar* (a sharper, almost cheddar-like white cheese), and *tulum peynir* (literally, cheese encased in a skin). When a leading newspaper ran a full-page article on "Turkey's Ten Best Cheeses," most of them were just variations on the Big Three. Turkish friends can rhapsodize about the texture of an exceptional *tulum peynir* or the creaminess of a favorite full-fat *beyaz peynir,* but most of these cheeses are, to my taste, pretty similar. My years in France spoiled me, I'm afraid. The Turkish dairy industry could easily support a variety to rival French cheeses, but the demand hasn't been there, at least not until recently.

Traditionally, Turks are not particularly adventurous eaters, but their travels abroad have created a taste and demand for new foods. Larger grocery stores now offer Turkish versions of cheddar and mozzarella and even a sliced cheese all too reminiscent of Velveeta. There are increasing offerings of imported cheeses (mostly Danish bleu, Emmenthal or Parmesan).

At the weekly market, there are mountains of the three traditional cheeses, but not much else. You can buy *kaşar* from several different villages, but it's all *kaşar*. The most popular cheese—eaten for breakfast, used in *börek*s, and essential with *rakı*—is *beyaz peynir*. You can get it full fat, half fat, or fat free, but feta is feta. You are more likely to convince Americans to give up their lattes than you are to get Turks to abandon *beyaz peynir*. No need to give it up, but why not more variety? Meanwhile, I encourage a young academic acquaintance who is doing research on new cheese varieties. If he'd like to start some Brie or Chaumes research, I might even give him a grant.

The weekly market on Heybeliada is not just for food. Each year the market grows larger, with some stalls on the side streets devoted to housewares and clothing. As I move along the first side street, one young girl is selling only handmade wooden spoons, the best of them made of boxwood. As a daily echo of the market, Mehmet, a housewares salesman, used to set up his tables every day, summer or winter, on the island's main street. Except Wednesday, of course, when he had a substantial presence at the market. In difficult economic times, he was on to something. He had no overhead, could stay home if the weather was bad, and would gladly "special order" anything needed. If he didn't have it on hand, he'd find it on the mainland and bring it the next day. I always looked forward to his smiling face and entrepreneurial spirit. His death last year left a void in island life.

The market is lively. It is colorful. But the offerings depend largely on what the farmers are raising in Yalova. The one constant is that everything is fresh and bursting with flavor. Who could ask for anything more? The most common foods in Turkey—all plentiful at our weekly market—are the cornerstones of the healthy Mediterranean diet: olive oil, garlic, tomatoes, peppers, zucchini, artichokes, spinach and other greens, okra, leeks, root vegetables, lentils, beans, peas, grains, aromatic herbs and spices.

At first I was frustrated by the seasonal limitations. Americans have gotten used to having any fruit or vegetable at any time of year…even if it has to come from South America and even if it has little flavor when it arrives. The island market may not offer cherries in December, but for traditional Mediterranean food in its purest seasonal simplicity, I defy anyone to find produce better or fresher than the offerings on Heybeliada. A summer tomato from Yalova bursts with flavor that is only a childhood memory, if that, to most Americans.

XIX
DAILY BREAD

The happiness of man…much depends on dinner.
Lord Byron, *Don Juan*

Turkish cuisine can be boring and repetitive or exciting and varied—it all depends on where you're eating and who's in the kitchen—but it's difficult to find a truly bad meal. Not surprisingly, some of the best and most unusual cuisine is found in Turkish homes. When Sevin was staying with us for a few days, her approach to cooking was not only inventive but also as thrifty as her approach to legal fees. She offered to make a spinach *börek* (a filled pastry something like Greek *spanokopita*), so I volunteered to be her sous-chef. After washing the spinach leaves and trimming off the stems and roots, I was about to toss the debris in the garbage when Sevin cried, "No! I'm using them," as she proceeded to make a wonderfully tangy salad of olive oil, lemon juice, and the discarded bits of spinach stem. When we eat at her house, nearly every dish is something I've never seen before.

Too many restaurants, especially those catering to the tourist trade, focus on a few easy-to-make, familiar dishes. Why bother making something complicated, they reason, if customers aren't going to appreciate it? Luckily, there are others that make the effort to offer enticing and unusual flavors and textures. Heybeliada's restaurants along the seafront mostly specialize in *meze* and fish, but a few can also conjure up lamb dishes fit for a sultan's table. Since the island's restaurateurs hail from a number of different regions, their offerings reflect regional specialties and offer some variety when we feel like eating out.

Mostly, though, we cook at home. I can't resist the fresh, colorful produce at the weekly market. In our early island days, I fought an uphill battle trying to cook the way I might in San Francisco. Turks are fairly conservative eaters, and many foods Americans take for granted are not part of Turkish tradition. Just as some basic Turkish ingredients can't be found in American supermarkets, many foods that seem essential to Americans are simply not available in Turkey. Some can be found in gourmet shops in Beyoğlu, Bebek, or other Istanbul districts with large expatriate populations, but that does me little good on Heybeliada. Our most welcome American guests are those who bring us chunky peanut butter. The bright side is that the city's grocers are becoming more and more cosmopolitan. Or perhaps their customers are becoming more demanding. Whatever the reason, items that used to be rarities (broccoli, tofu, Arborio rice) are now produced locally.

Ben and I spent a long time fruitlessly searching for Italian basil and fresh coriander, but finally gave up the hunt. We found a source for seeds, but nearly despaired of finding the right spot to grow them. It wasn't that the soil was wrong. The problem was the stray cats. They liked the soft bed of green in pots—so much more comfortable than the chilly soil—and the herbs were flattened and unusable. Finally the pots were moved to a small greenhouse where they produced generous yields. Just as I managed to grow basil successfully, it began appearing in Turkish markets.

For many years, our jobs kept us on the move—three years here, two years there—with never a chance to develop a garden. Sometimes we might have a few small pots of herbs in a kitchen, but Heybeliada offered our first chance to have a serious herb garden. There is something irresistible about strolling from the kitchen to the terrace to pick fresh mint, rosemary, oregano, bay, or whatever we need for that evening's meal.

Our Greek friend, Niko, suggested foraging beyond our own garden. My urban soul would never have thought of looking farther than the weekly market, but Niko introduced us to some of the wild edibles on the island. In spring, Heybeli's hills are a treasure trove of wild asparagus. It is also the season for fresh garlic, something I had never used before. Though I find it too mild for many dishes, fresh garlic is the perfect accompaniment to the delicate wild asparagus. Niko tossed the asparagus stalks and garlic cloves in a bit of olive oil, rolled them around while sautéing for a bit, and let the thinnest asparagus stalks disintegrate into the sauce. A dollop of red wine enhanced the mix, and, just before removing the pan from the fire, he finished off with another drizzle of olive oil. It's lucky that not all islanders know about the asparagus. So far, there's plenty for those who do.

Other islanders have been generous with recipes, most of which are simple, offer only rough measurements, and produce exquisite results. Most of the foodie cookbooks popular in San Francisco are useless to us here. Their ever more far-fetched ingredients are simply impossible to find. Turkish cookbooks let us experiment with recipes for our own day-to-day needs, but I don't have the chutzpah to make Turkish dishes for Turkish dinner guests. Particularly not for the neighbor who owns one of the best restaurants in central Istanbul. For those occasions, I rely on Mediterranean cookbooks that use simple, classic ingredients. In my island kitchen, Paula Wolfert and Claudia Roden are goddesses. Their recipes are based on the wonderful, simple Mediterranean ingredients we can easily find, but use them with a non-Turkish flair.

Sometimes our Mediterranean accent is Italian, sometimes French, occasionally Spanish or North African. Sometimes we go farther afield. For a Southern meal of mint juleps, New Orleans red beans and rice and a sort-of *étouffé*, I carefully avoided buying pork sausage (though it is available in Istanbul) since I wasn't entirely sure that all the guests, however secular, were willing to eat pork.

My mistake. They were all disappointed and made me promise to do it again the *right* way.

Though many Turks think they like only Turkish food, they sometimes discover they're wrong. Kadri was not looking forward to an evening of Indian food. He explained that he doesn't like garlic or hot spices, but would eat what he could. He repeated this at the table as he reached for his second large helping of vindaloo.

As we have become more accustomed to cooking Turkish food, our kitchen staples have changed. Beans and lentils take up a lot of room in our Heybeliada kitchen. I get a warm glow just looking at the colorful lineup of glass jars with dry garbanzo, cranberry, fava, haricot, black, and other beans, along with red and brown lentils and even some yellow Indian *chana dal* I found at a market in the city.

The variety of Turkish uses for beans and lentils has been a revelation, giving me new respect for the red lentil (*mercimek*), an item little used in Western cuisine. It is a humble, even self-effacing legume. Simple red lentil soup is a village and working class staple, the perfect breakfast on a cold morning or the Turkish equivalent of chicken soup, good for whatever ails you. Added to a stew or soup, the red lentils quietly disappear, making an ideal thickener with far more nutrition than a flour paste would provide. The red lentil can also move center stage and play a leading role, as in *mercimek köftesi*, a spicy mix of lentils, bulgur, onions, red pepper, and parsley, shaped into finger-sized servings. It has become one of my standard dishes.

I am lucky enough to have a husband who loves to cook. Ben produces wonderful Indian dishes and works magic with beans of all kinds. But the Heybeli kitchen has also become the laboratory for his latest obsession: pickle making.

Though he hates grocery shopping, Ben usually accompanies me to the market on Wednesdays to help carry things home. He knows I am likely to overbuy when I see the beautiful produce. In *badem* season, though, he is the one eager to go. Certain cucumbers are called *badem* (almond) because they are small and crunchy enough to use for making pickles. Traditionally, the best pickles are made in Çengelköy, a village on the Asian side of the Bosphorus, where our friends Belma and Sami live; they brought some of the delicacy to us and got Ben interested in trying it himself. About that time, he also found an article on pickle making in *Cornucopia: Turkey for Connoisseurs,* a wonderful English-language magazine about Turkish history, life, and arts. He became possessed by pickle frenzy. Huge jars were purchased, along with coarse rock salt. During *badem* season, our windowsill is filled with pickles in varying stages of readiness.

He soon found that there is a quiet *turşucu* (pickle maker) passion among Turks. University professors, lawyers, accountants, all sorts of Turks love to make pickles and are ready to compare notes about when and where to find the best *badem* or which tricks and secrets will ensure the best pickles. Nermin, our housekeeper, was amused at the idea of a foreign man thinking he could make decent pickles. She looked at his work, smiled wanly, and pointed out the white scum on top. The secret? Add a couple of raw chickpeas. And don't put the pickles near the sun. But *Cornucopia* advised the opposite: put the jar in a window with good exposure. It would take some trial and error, it seemed.

While visiting a university in central Turkey, Ben happened to mention that he is a hobby *turşucu*. The vice rector, the dean, the head of the English department: each turned out to be a devoted *turşucu*. This was the richest information lode of all. The real secret to keeping the pickles clear, they insisted, is to add a few mustard seeds.

The problem, however, is that most of these *turşu* aficionados are middle-aged and under strict orders from their doctors to avoid salt. As a result, most of the pickles have to be given away. Friends are happy to receive them the first time, but somehow look less delighted the ninth or tenth time. Pickle making is the Turkish equivalent of growing zucchini in summer. You can have a fine crop, but can't get rid of it. Maybe Ben should open a stand at the market. There doesn't seem to be a *turşucu* there yet.

******

Some vegetables come and go with the seasons, of course, but if there is one single vegetable staple in Turkey, it is eggplant (*patlıcan*), a vegetable I remember despising as a child. There is a saying that a Turkish village girl should not be married until she knows at least 100 ways to prepare eggplant. If a Turk began reciting eggplant dishes as Forrest Gump's pal, Bubba, started naming shrimp dishes, the Turk would just be warming up by the time Bubba ran out of ideas.

At one *meze* table we sometimes find four or five eggplant dishes, maybe *patlıcan ızgara,* sautéed with peppers and served with yogurt on the side; or *patlıcan soslu,* chunks of grilled eggplant in a tomato sauce; or *patlıcan salatası,* smoked and pureed with lemon, yogurt, and garlic; maybe even *imam bayıldı* ("the imam swooned"), half an eggplant stuffed with vegetables sautéed in olive oil (one story says the imam swooned because it was so delicious; another because the olive oil was so expensive); or *patlıcan közde,* fragrant with garlic.

The hot dishes with eggplant are even better than the cold ones. My own favorite is the incomparable *beğendi*, a wonderfully refined Ottoman puree of smoked eggplant, butter, and cheese served as a bed for fork-tender pieces of lamb. I can never resist a small restaurant, Haci Salih, just off Istanbul's busy Istiklal Avenue, where I know I can get the world's best *beğendi*. It is nearly always on the menu and never fails to satisfy. I thought it would be impossible to find on Heybeliada, where fish is king, but the simple little Ada Restaurant turned out to specialize in a lighter, lower-cholesterol variation called *alinazik*. My passion for *beğendi* puts me in good company. Empress Eugenie, wife of Napoleon III, was so entranced by her taste of *beğendi* when visiting Sultan Abdül Aziz that she sent her chef to the palace kitchen for lessons. The sultan's chef refused to divulge his recipe.

Turks are devoted meat eaters and can work unexpected magic with foods we didn't know we could like. Even liver—probably the most hated meat in America—can be sublime when prepared by a Turkish chef. Although the town of Bolu is famed for its master chefs, it is Edirne, the former Adrianopolis, near the Greek border, that might be called the liver capital of Turkey. Edirne is famous for small, simple restaurants that serve delicate, paper-thin fried liver…and little else. At least once a year, an American friend proposes an excursion to Edirne. Once we are settled into her favorite liver joint, we always toast our mothers, who would either faint or die laughing if they knew we'd driven more than two hours just to eat liver.

When island friends invite us for dinner, particularly in summer when we can sit outdoors, the menu is usually a few *meze* followed by grilled meat. In colder weather, it might be one of the hearty stews or bean dishes that could be called Turkish comfort food. Just as Americans abroad might pine for Mom's spaghetti and meat balls, a homesick Turk will yearn for a steaming dish of *kuru fasulye*, white haricot beans cooked with lamb, tomatoes, onions, herbs and spices.

What goes on a Turkish dinner table depends on location, on economic level, on time available for cooking, on personal preference. But all Turks agree on one thing: bread is essential at any meal. Every culture has its staff of life—rice in China, potatoes in Ireland, bread in Turkey.

Turkish bread, *ekmek,* is available fresh several times a day from neighborhood bakeries, and each household sends someone (often the smallest child) to buy multiple loaves for each meal. *Ekmek* looks the same throughout the country, comes unsliced, and always has a light, fresh aroma. No one would dream of eating bread more than a few hours old, but wasting bread is considered shameful, so stale pieces are put out for birds or other creatures. In every restaurant, the waiter will bring a basket of *ekmek* slices immediately. No matter what else a Turk may order, he will want plenty of *ekmek.*

An island neighbor wanted to lose a few kilos; his wife was complaining about his weight and he could barely close the buttons on his shirts. Convinced that all Americans are diet experts, he asked for our advice. Ben and I thought the Atkins low-carbohydrate approach would be best since he wanted fast results. We explained the rules: plenty of lean protein, some leafy vegetables, but, in the first stage, only thirty grams of carbohydrate per day. Two thin slices from a loaf of *ekmek* would easily take him beyond that limit, so we told him the bad news:

"No bread."

He was puzzled. "So, only three or four pieces at breakfast?"

"No," we replied, "None. Zero."

We had to go over this several times. It was simply not a concept he could grasp. How could anyone eat a meal with *no* bread at all? His buttons are ready to pop, his wife's complaints grow louder, but there has never been another mention of dieting.

Ask anyone in Istanbul, though, and you will hear that today's *ekmek* is inferior to the old *ekmek*. This is not just nostalgia. They are right. It has been refined and has lost its traditional chewy texture and sourdough flavor. Real *ekmek* does exist, but you have to look for it. Sometimes it is found only in more remote towns that haven't "improved" the recipe yet.

Many Turks would gag on anything but classic *ekmek,* but the more adventurous now demand variety. In response, some bakeries are producing just about anything from olive loaves to baguettes, from challah to whole-grain. Even on our small island, we have seen the changes. There are two rival bakers. One has remained faithful to the traditional *ekmek.* The other decided to test the market for other breads. He began offering whole wheat, oatmeal, rye, and even the seductively aromatic flat bread, *pide,* normally available only during Ramazan, when it is used to break the fast at sunset. At first he overestimated islanders' willingness to try something new, but adjusted his production to meet the limited demand. His main business remains the traditional *ekmek,* but he is gradually building a larger market for non-traditional breads. We are among his most devoted customers.

******

Istanbul is a superb restaurant city. Turkish cuisine prevails, of course, but international offerings include Chinese, Japanese, Italian, French, Greek, Thai, Mexican and more. On the island, we're restricted to Turkish options, but there's plenty of variety.

Some food writers argue that there are three great cuisines: French, Chinese, and Turkish. The more I learn about Turkish food, the more I'm inclined to agree.

The Ottoman Empire spread across a lot of culinary traditions, many of which made their way into Turkish cuisine. Since our Heybeliada restaurant owners come from different regions, their offerings vary accordingly. Some of my favorite dishes suggest the range: the thick, rich yogurt of the Turkic nomads; *beğendi* (smoked eggplant puree) from the Ottoman court; *çerkez tavuk* (Circassian chicken), an appetizer of chicken, walnuts, and garlic, borrowed from the Caucasus; *çıpura,* simply grilled fresh bream from the Aegean Sea; and *künefe*, an impossibly rich cheese-filled baklava-like pastry from the Arab-influenced southeast. All can be found on Heybeliada.

In the city, we have a favorite *meyhane* (the unpretentious restaurants dedicated to good food and drink). There are few things more satisfying than a long *meyhane* evening with a congenial group of gourmands. And a good *meyhane* will do just about anything for its regular customers. When friends, or friends of friends, pass through Istanbul, we often go with them to our favorite *meyhane*. It has been the site of some of our best Istanbul evenings, and visitors are usually glad to learn something about Turkish cuisine beyond kebabs.

One frequent visitor is a Belgian friend, Georges, always a pleasure to dine with and, like us, more gourmand than gourmet. One summer, he was in town at the same time as a San Franciscan we know slightly, Toni, who was traveling with her mother. We spoke with Toni on the phone, making arrangements for that evening's dinner at our favorite *meyhane* in Beyoğlu. Our first hint of trouble was when the mother, a Montessori teacher in Marin County, icily stated, "I am a very strict vegetarian."

OK, no problem. Turkey, with its vast selection of *meze*, is a paradise for vegetarians. But we didn't like the tone. Later, Georges called to see if we could get together that evening. We explained about the two women, but he said he'd love to join us and meet them. We warned him that it might not be a good idea. He pooh-poohed the notion, so we all met at the appointed hour.

At the restaurant, Osman had reserved our favorite table, which already had *rakı*, water, and ice waiting for us. He smiled broadly as he asked our guests, *"Ne içersiniz?"* ("What would you like to drink?")

Georges ordered a bottle of one of Turkey's best white wines. Toni said she'd try a glass of that, too. Her mother, however, said, "One glass of chardonnay." Osman looked at us for guidance. We explained to her that Turkish white wines were pretty much just dry or sweet, but recommended two that we particularly like. (Only in the last year or two have boutique wineries started producing a full range of varietals.)

"No. I drink only chardonnay," she said firmly.

"Well, they don't have any, but try the one Georges ordered. It's excellent."

She tried it. Didn't like it. "Oh, never mind. I'll just have soy milk."

I translated for Osman, who couldn't believe his ears. Milk made out of soybeans? Why would anyone drink such a thing at a *meyhane*? Or anywhere, for that matter? But he smiled at her and simply said, *"Kalmadı."*

"Too bad, they seem to have run out," I translated, not bothering to tell her that "None left" often means they never had it anyway.

By then the *meze* platter had arrived, filled with glorious vegetarian delights: smoky eggplant salad, fresh green beans in olive oil, artichoke hearts with tiny cubes of potato and carrot, *haydari* (thick, herbed yogurt), *fava* (a paste of broad beans with dill), *ezme* (a fiery salsa-like tomato dish), and more exotic fare like *topik* (a slightly sweet Armenian dumpling). White cheese (that familiar *beyaz peynir,* Turkey's feta) and fresh melon, the traditional starters for *rakı* drinkers, were automatically placed on the table for us.

Montessori Mom toyed with a couple of them, but nothing pleased her. Trying to remain the gracious hosts, Ben and I asked if there was something else she might like. We already knew she wasn't going to want the succulent grilled fish that awaited us after the *meze*.

"An omelet," she demanded.

Again, Osman didn't know where to look. But, for regular customers, he was willing to do what he could and wanted everyone to be happy. "How about some *menemen?*" he suggested to us, referring to a Turkish concoction of scrambled eggs with jalapeno-hot *sivri* peppers and tomatoes.

"Sure," we told him in desperation. "Let's give it a try."

The *menemen* arrived a little later, and I couldn't help wondering what words had been exchanged in the kitchen. *Menemen* is not what a *meyhane* is for.

I tried not to watch what she was doing, but couldn't help myself. She moved it around on the plate a bit, wrinkled her nose, and pushed it aside, saying, "Awfully runny."

Osman, afraid that he had failed, asked us if he could do something. I explained that she thought it was runny. "I'll have it cooked some more," he offered.

"Never mind," we assured him, as Georges whispered into my ear, "*Quelle emmerdeuse!*" and made an excuse about needing to get back to his hotel for an important phone call. "Coward! I warned you," I whispered back.

Still oblivious, our Marin County matron waved a friendly goodbye, said she was ready to go, too, and asked if there was someplace on the way back to her hotel where she could find that soy milk. I wondered why she bothers to travel. Why not just stay home? She'd be happier and so would Osman.

******

Whenever we return from a trip, the first night's meal is usually at one of the island restaurants. We had just returned from several weeks in the United States and wanted to catch up on island gossip. From the airport we called Uğur and Inci to see if they could meet us for dinner when we arrived on an evening ferry. They said fine.

As the ferry rounded Papaz Hill and we were within sight of the pier, we called again so they could start down the hill from their house. Each of our island friends and neighbors has a favorite restaurant. Uğur's is Balıkhane ("Fish House"), so we were waiting there for them at an outside table.

As its name suggests, this restaurant, owned by the island's fishmonger, has fish and pretty much only fish. The waiter brought a few salads and vegetable *meze,* but particularly recommended that day's hot hors-d'oeuvres (called *ara sıcak,* literally a "hot interval" between the cold *meze* and the main course). It was hard to decide between fried and grilled calamari, so we asked for both. Along with that came a buttery shrimp, cheese, and hot chili dish (*karides güveç*) served in individual casseroles. Uncharacteristically, we left the *ara sıcak* at that, resisting the tempting descriptions of the day's *börek* choices, flaky pastries filled with meat, cheese, or vegetables. There is no requirement in Turkish restaurants to move beyond the *meze* and *ara sıcak.* Many Turkish diners spend a long evening talking, drinking, and nibbling their *meze,* never bothering with a main course.

But we had just returned and were longing for Turkish grilled fish. San Francisco's petrale sole and Dungeness crab are ambrosial, but they are something completely different. In Turkey, fish is serious, yet simple. The simplicity is in the preparation—most often grilled and served with lemon, red onion, and a sprig or two of arugula. The seriousness is in the range of fish available and the terms for them. Not content with a single name for fish, Turks distinguish stages of development with different names. One of the most popular fish is bluefish, called *lüfer* when it is at its optimum size. But its names are, in ascending order of size, *defne yaprağı* ("bay leaf"), *çinakop, sarı kanat, lüfer,* and *kafane.*

Turkey's four seas, as well as its lakes and rivers, provide a range of fresh fish unavailable anywhere else I can think of. But even this can't satisfy the Turkish hunger for fish. More than once I have seen deliveries to Heybeliada of large cartons of frozen calamari, clearly marked "Product of India."

Balıkhane Restaurant gets the pick of the fishermen's catch each day, so we asked the waiter to advise us. He recited the choices, including a few non-local options, but his firm recommendation was a skewer of grilled *iskorpit*, the black scorpion fish known as *rascasse* in France, where it is a vital ingredient in the best *bouillabaisse*. On Heybeliada, it's the cheapest fish on offer, and meltingly delicious.

As we finished the meal with small porcelain cups of Turkish coffee, Uğur reminded us that it was the Ottomans who introduced coffee to Europe. But French cafes owe a double debt to the Ottomans, who also introduced the notion of outdoor restaurants. For centuries, *Istanbullu* diners have preferred their meals along the waterfront, in courtyards with the sounds of fountains, or on hillsides overlooking restful scenery. With the exception of some simple fast-food places, nearly every restaurant on Heybeliada fits that description. But, as this evening proved to us once again, even more important than the setting and cuisine is the notion of a relaxed, unhurried meal, savoring both the food and the fellowship.

As the evening waned, and we watched the last of the ferryboats glide toward the pier, I relished the aftertaste of a fine but simple meal and the warm glow from the evening's *rakı* and lively conversation. I thought about that first ferryboat that brought me to look at houses on the island and the many others we've traveled on since then. I remembered the second thoughts that haunted us immediately after buying the house and how our friendships with Ibrahim, Sevin, and Günhan grew from those early days. I summoned up memories of other evenings like this one with islanders who have become good friends. And I smiled to myself, thinking I should have some ruby slippers to click together, as I said out loud, "There's no place like home."

XX
WHOSE ISLAND IS THIS ANYWAY?

That is what islands are for; they are places where different destinies can meet and intersect in the full isolation of time.

Lawrence Durrell, *Bitter Lemons*

On a morning in early May, I am sitting on our front balcony with the day's second cup of coffee. It is a hazy morning, and the Asian side of Istanbul is invisible today. Without the distraction of that other shore, I can focus on our clear view of the Greek Orthodox seminary, just to the left, atop Papaz Hill's dense greenery. It is an imposing 19th century building with a Turkish flag flying from its red tile roof, and remains a reminder of this island's significant *Rum* (Greek) heritage though it has remained closed for more than thirty years.

At the same time, I am aware of the deep rumble of drums in the distance. The naval high school's cadets must be marching this morning. Even before the *Rum* era, the navy was a major presence on this island, and today still controls extensive parts of it. These cadets, victors in a highly competitive entrance process that takes only 200 of the more than 40,000 applicants each year, will go on to the naval academy and become the next generation of Turkish naval officers. This morning they are probably practicing for the May 19 Youth and Sports Day festivals.

Today is Thursday, so Nermin will soon arrive to clean our house and help us prepare for a guest we're expecting this weekend. Her extended Turkish family predates even many of the *Rum* who lived on this island. Her grandfather came to Heybeli more than 100 years ago and built a business bringing well water, by donkey, from Çam Limanı, the bay on the far side of the island, to the *Rum* households of the time. Since our house was built just over 100 years ago, its earliest *Rum* owners were probably his customers. The house was sold in the 1920s, when so many *Rum* left Istanbul, to a Navy family.

They, in turn, sold it to a middle-class Turkish family, who sold it to Bingül, who sold it to us. We are not only the next phase in this house's history, but also a throwback to the earliest residents. Just as the first owners bought water from Nermin's grandfather, we are customers of Nermin's cousin, who owns the franchise for one of the major water suppliers today. *Rum*, Navy, *Istanbullu*: all three are part of the tapestry of Heybeliada. But where do we fit in? Maybe in the island's oldest category of all: the exile.

Exile can be imposed or voluntary. The first exiles here were early Byzantine royals who ended up on the islands when deposed or out of favor. The tales of their imprisonment and mutilation are chilling. In the 20th century, Leon Trotsky spent the first five years of his exile, 1929-1933, on Büyükada, where the Turkish authorities thought he might be safest from assassination attempts. His biographer, Isaac Deutscher, tells us that Trotsky, despite initial misgivings, came to consider his years on the Princes' Islands "the calmest, the most creative, and the least unhappy time of his exile."

But in recent decades, the "exiles" have all been voluntary: those looking for a respite from the hubbub of the city, or, in our case, looking for the perfect retirement site, wherever in the world it turned out to be. "Exile" seems a harsh word to me, and "voluntary exile" almost a contradiction in terms, but people tend to look on the dark side of leaving one's native land. In fact, of course, the decision to live in another country doesn't necessarily mean a rejection of one's roots. "Expatriate" does not mean "ex-patriot."

Some of our American friends refuse to believe that someone might enjoy living outside the United States. "Don't you get homesick?" they ask. Or sometimes they're more indirect: "What do you miss most about the U.S. when you're in Turkey?" Only persiflage can answer questions like that, so my stock answer used to be "800 numbers and NPR." Now I need a new response. Our U.S. bank's 800 number is toll-free even from Heybeliada. And we listen online not only to NPR, but also to San Francisco's classical radio station, KDFC.

We're content here. Along with the comfortable, familiar side of life, there is the less-familiar, but always entrancing exotic side. Expatriate life seems to require not just a willingness, but a strong desire to step out of oneself, to try on other world views and ways of living and thinking. In a May 2006 *New Yorker* article about Patrick Leigh Fermor, a colorful character and skilled writer who has spent much of his life in Greece, Anthony Lane wrote: "...he exults in the otherness of the far-flung place—in the precise degree to which [it does] not resemble the contours, moral and geological, of his native land. He demands nothing from [it] save an opportunity to slip quietly under [its] skin." This is a beautiful explanation of the appeal of expatriate life. It's not for everyone, but for those drawn to it, it is irresistible.

In fact, we're not the only "expatriates" or "exiles" on Heybeliada. We're not *Rum* or Navy or deeply rooted *Istanbullu*, but, then, neither are most of the other islanders these days. Finding a native *Istanbullu* is becoming as hard as finding a native San Franciscan. After many years of being out of fashion, the islands are attracting more attention, and real estate is beginning to boom. The more modern side of Heybeliada makes it a comfortable place to live, and the enduring flavor of an older Istanbul gives it much of its charm. The wooden villas, the absence of cars, the slower pace, and the *komşuluk* (neighborliness) all contribute to this and attract new residents, new "voluntary exiles." There are plentiful traces of the earlier *Rum* character of the island and of the more than 230-year naval tradition on Heybeliada. But most of today's population has little in common with those Heybeli islanders of earlier days. Ben and I are among a bare handful of foreigners here, but even among the *Rum* and Turks, Heybeli's residents are a motley group.

Heybeli, like Turkey, is 99% Muslim, so it is a bit startling to see a bearded Greek Orthodox priest in his long, black *rasso* walking along the seafront or buying vegetables at the market. He may be from the theological school atop Papaz Hill or from St. George monastery on Büyükada, or even visiting from Mt. Athos in Greece. To a Turkish islander, he might seem a ghost from the past. The *Rum* roots on this island are deep, but there is little left but roots. Many of the *Rum* left in the 1920s, the early years of the Turkish republic, during the "exchange of populations" mandated by the Lausanne Treaty. More departed in the aftermath of the September 1955 riots in Istanbul over the Cyprus issue. Even among the two-dozen Greeks now part of this island's year-round population, not all are *Rum*. Some, like our friends Niko and Vasiliki, are from Greece, with no family roots in Istanbul. Even so, Niko, like the remaining *Rum* islanders, is passionate about preserving Heybeliada's *Rum* legacy: from the impeccably maintained Greek Orthodox theological school and library to the neglected and deserted Greek primary school, from the quiet simplicity of Terk-i Dünya monastery to the splendor of the finest mansions built for *Rum* owners.

During the time we have been on Heybeli, we have observed a deepening of Greek-Turkish cooperation and friendship. Business groups are exchanging delegations and forming sister-city relationships. Musical groups, especially Niko's Bosphorus, are creating a fusion of Greek and Turkish traditional music. There is serious talk of reopening the Greek Orthodox seminary. More and more Greek tourists are coming to revisit and relive the days when the *Rumlar* were a major presence on the islands. The local restaurants have taken note and, ever alert to the market, now offer menus in Greek and even *ouzo* as well as *rakı*.

The legacy of the non-Muslim minorities is one of the special qualities and heritages of all of the Princes' Islands, but only Heybeliada can also claim the long presence of the Turkish Navy. Large chunks of the island are Navy property, guarded by young Army conscripts and inaccessible to any but authorized personnel.

The cadets at the naval high school are as much a part of the island scene as the seagulls and horse carriages. They are unmistakable in their uniforms: black for winter, sparkling white for summer. Rarely seen alone, they stay together in small groups, nearly always in uniform, and seldom in contact with island residents.

We have never yet succeeded in visiting the naval high school facilities, though we would love to see the small Byzantine church still standing on the grounds of the upper campus. Occasionally we meet one of the teachers at an island restaurant or teashop, but in terms of human contact, the naval presence has little impact on our day-to-day life. Our only reminders are the drums accompanying their marches, a walking trail that suddenly ends at fenced military property, or the roar of a Navy-owned passenger van along what is usually a quiet pedestrian road.

In fact, our lives have little in common with the Greek Orthodox priests or the Turkish naval officers. Their interests, their activities are far removed from ours. We fall in more naturally with some of the longtime *Istanbullu*s who share our love of the city's cultural life and whose careers and life experiences are more similar to ours. We can try, like Leigh Fermor, to "slip quietly under their skin," but even with them, of course, we are still something apart, never fully part of their society.

I remember one time when this struck me full force. We were invited to Ibrahim's house for lunch one Sunday in late August. Kadri and Nilgün were there, as well as a retired naval officer, one of Ibrahim's former colleagues and someone the rest of us had not met before. For some reason, Ben and I were a bit late. As we walked down the hill toward Ibrahim's apartment, the skies opened with one of the late August downpours we never seem to expect. We grew up in California where it never rains in summer.

By the time we reached Ibrahim's, we were soaked. Everyone was inside and deep into conversation. The four Turks, all from longtime Istanbul families, had discovered a treasure trove of mutual acquaintances and old school friends, even relatives they didn't know they had in common. As we sat, still wet, in the now chilly air, we tried to keep up with what they were saying. Names, relationships, marriages, divorces were reviewed or revealed amidst "what ever happened to…" and "didn't you know about…" and "remember the time when…" and half-finished anecdotes that elicited roars of laughter. Wet, cold, miserable, and sharing none of these memories, I felt a momentary pang of rootlessness and indulged in a brief flush of self-pity. What *are* we doing here? I asked myself.

But soon we were dry again, the returning sun brought songbirds, Ibrahim took over the barbecue grill, and the conversation turned to other things. That momentary wave of melancholy was soon conquered by the realization that those differences are not the point. I smiled to myself as I remembered a tongue-in-cheek Turkish toast that is used when friends are enjoying a good meal and each other's company: "May our worst days be like this one!" Maybe this one really was.

Heybeliada is a place where all of us, whatever our roots and backgrounds, find a way to come together. We may not share those early *Istanbullu* ties, but neither do the Turks who have moved here from Izmir or Ankara or Gaziantep. We'll never speak perfect Turkish, but, then, neither will the Greeks. And the naval cadets will soon move on, with Heybeliada becoming only one chapter in their lives, a time to recall in later years with navy colleagues who will also have passed this way.

We can take a sort of comfort in a line from Orhan Pamuk's *Istanbul: Memories of a City*: "Istanbul is a place where, for the past hundred and fifty years, no one has been able to feel completely at home."

Istanbul grew from a population of one million in the mid-1950s to some fifteen million today. In the older, smaller Istanbul, members of the elite class all knew each other, went to school together, married each other. They felt a sense of ownership of the city and find today's megalopolis a divided place, with tensions between tradition and Western influence, between the established elite and a flood of impoverished newcomers, between those with Istanbul roots and those who don't share their history. Even the guests at Ibrahim's lunch may feel, from time to time, that they don't fully belong to this new Istanbul.

But we are all part of the island's tapestry, part of this little world suspended between old and new Istanbul. Some have been here longer, some know more of the history, some are more active in local affairs, some are Turkish and some are not...but all are hopelessly addicted to this little archipelago. Among ourselves, we may argue that one or the other island is superior to the others, but when confronted with non-islanders, we revert to our insular solidarity, smug and snug in our voluntary exile, and recognizing each other as fellow addicts. Just as Ben and I try to slip under their skin, they are welcoming and accepting enough to try to slip under ours. The island itself becomes our bond. "May our worst days be like this one!" We can't complain.

XXI
OTHER ISLANDERS

Say Istanbul and a seagull comes to mind
Half silver and half foam, half fish and half bread...
        Bedri Rahmi Eyüpoğlu, "The Saga of Istanbul"

One evening, as we were finishing the second round of *rakı* with island neighbors in our garden, one of our guests presented a challenge: What makes a true *adalı* (islander)? Not surprisingly, no one selected an ethnic or national identity as part of the formula.

"Being born on the island is essential!" was the immediate response from the only one of us who fits that description. We rejected his definition as self-serving.

"Year-round residents only!" said another. Some difference of opinion.

I liked a third suggestion: the true islander is one who does something (restores a house; prevents a forest fire) to preserve the island's beauty. When it came to my turn, however, I had to admit that none of us could make the grade. For me, the quintessential *adalı* is the *martı,* the seagull. Once we accepted non-human candidates, others voted for the island's street cats.

"Even the stray dogs may have better claim to true *adalı* status than some of the people who spend time here," insisted one of our grumpier neighbors.

I still vote for the gulls. When I am away from Heybeliada, it is the seagulls I miss the most. They are so essential to the island environment that Zeyyat, the short story writer, titled one of his books *Seagull Island,* as a fictional name for the island he depicted. It turns out that the seagulls may, indeed, be the oldest islanders, predating even the Byzantine monks. In early times, there were no seagulls in central Istanbul, along the Bosphorus. They were only on the islands.

The first sound in the morning on Heybeliada is the cry of seagulls. And they continue their calls throughout the day. Although I grew up in the San Francisco Bay Area, where there are plenty of seagulls, none of them ever had much to say. These are a different breed. They, like the Turks, love to talk. The seagulls are everywhere; it is impossible to imagine the island without them. They watch from rooftops, they settle along the shore, they sometimes walk along the main street. They have no fear of anyone or anything. And when one of them discovers something of interest (usually food) or sees danger lurking, the alarm is passed from one to another, with dozens of gulls gathering together at the site, circling around the find. They keep their distance from humans, but with an eye always on possible sources of food.

In the spring, seagulls are on every roof, standing guard over their nests. Ben and I watch the babies as they learn to fly. The mothers are relentless, keeping the hesitant youngsters hard at work practicing their lessons. When young seagulls make that first flight, they usually aren't yet strong enough to fly back up to the nest, and spend a week or two on the ground until their wings develop a bit more. They can be seen along the roads, in gardens, or settled along the water's edge, with their parents close by keeping an eye on them.

One slow learner fell onto our terrace, unable to get out again. We considered somehow catching him and carrying him someplace where his parents could retrieve him, but decided to leave him alone for a while. At first he cowered in the ivy where he couldn't be seen,.

but changed his mind when our two resident stray cats took too much interest. They, too, kept their distance and had no intention of harming him. They were soon bored with him and moved on.

When we had nearly given up hope that he'd find a way out, the young seagull began climbing up the narrow steps to the flat roof above our kitchen. He thumped from one step to the next, complaining at each jump, sounding like a spoiled teenager who has been told to walk home from the mall. From there he made his way across to the roof of the house where his parents could now get to him. We thought this would be the last of him, but next day there was a thud, then a skittering racket on the small greenhouse nearby. The same young seagull was slipping around on the glass, unable to get the traction needed to fly away. He finally stumbled back onto the roof, but soon returned and slipped around again. At first I thought he simply didn't understand, but he kept coming back again and again, happy as a skateboarder.

******

The stray cats and dogs also have good claim to *adalı* status. The dogs are a remnant of an old Istanbul phenomenon, one that has mostly disappeared in the city. Foreign visitors in the 19th and early 20th century frequently wrote about the dogs of Istanbul, a significant presence in the city. At that time there were 40-50,000 dogs in the city—some commentators estimate twice that or more—but none had specific owners. Istanbul was, and to a large extent still is, a city of defined neighborhoods. The dogs acted as sentries. They knew who belonged and who didn't, and would send up an alarm if a stranger intruded at night. In return, the residents left scraps to feed them. Occasionally a wealthier resident might build a shelter or a water trough for them. But the dogs didn't belong to anyone.

The islands have long been associated with the dogs of Istanbul. Twice during the 19th century, there were attempts to rid the city of the dogs. Sultan Mahmut II tried to exile the dogs to Sivri, a small island visible from Heybeliada. When the boat was loaded and on its way, however, a sudden storm blew it off course onto the Asian shore. This was seen as a sign from God, and the dogs came back.

Mahmut II was able to abolish the powerful Janissary army. He was even able to outlaw the turban and introduce the fez. But he couldn't get rid of the city's dogs.

Toward the end of the 19th century, another Sultan, Abdül Aziz, again ordered the exile of the city's dogs to Sivri. This time the dogs were duly abandoned on the island, but when a series of fires broke out in several parts of Istanbul, people feared that this was divine retribution for the mistreatment of the animals. The dogs were once again returned to the city.

Other attempts to eradicate the ever-growing dog population followed in the early 20th century, but it was finally modernization and urban change that did them in. At the same time, some households began to keep dogs, but the Koran considers the dog to be a dirty animal, so the more conservative homes kept them outdoors. Only recently has Western-style ownership of pedigreed dogs become an *Istanbullu* fashion. But as with many Western habits, once introduced it burst forth full blown. Where once a pet dog inside the house was a rarity, today there are pet shops filled with dog toys, puppies, and an array of specialized foods for the pampered pooch.

On Heybeliada, stray dogs are still very much in evidence, but don't provide the neighborhood guard service of their mainland ancestors. They live in the woods and eat what they can find. Although Islam doesn't encourage keeping dogs indoors, it does require compassion toward all creatures. Island residents leave food for the dogs along the forest trails—leftover bread or rice or bones or whatever may be available. The dogs travel together in small groups, but I have never heard of anyone being attacked or harmed by them. They are mostly timid and easily chased away by a word or raised hand. Even so, Ben always carries a walking stick...just in case. When the packs are together, we can hear them howling in response to the *muezzin's* call to prayer from the mosque's minaret.

Some of the dogs have inherited the instinct for guarding humans, and a few island residents have adopted and trained young strays. They are the lucky ones. Although the dogs eat well during the summer, the less populated winter months can be difficult for them. Worried about possible disease and trying to reduce the numbers of dogs, the city authorities joined with humane societies and dog-loving islanders to begin a program of catching, inoculating, and sterilizing the dogs, giving each one an ear tag as proof of health. It has been successful so far. There seem to be fewer dogs, and residents feel a bit more comfortable around the tagged dogs. It is far better than taking them to a deserted island to starve.

Cats, on the other hand, are a very different case. Islamic tradition looks much more favorably on cats, and there is a story that the Prophet Mohammed once cut off his sleeve to avoid disturbing a cat sleeping on top of it. The dogs of Istanbul may be mostly gone, but cats have replaced them throughout the city. There is no attempt to control their numbers. On the islands, too, they are omnipresent. They multiply in spring and thrive in summer, when they are well fed by the larger vacation population. But when winter comes, many don't survive. The smart ones move to the seaside, near the fishermen, sleeping on their nets and waiting for scraps from the day's catch.

The island cats, like the dogs, belong to no one in particular. One scruffy stray turned up on our terrace a couple of years ago, an adolescent cat at that time. He entertained us by climbing and balancing on the grape arbor and was rewarded with bowls of food. Before long, he brought along a friend. We soon learned, though, that we were only one of the stops on their daily rounds. These, like cats around the world, are sybarites, looking for the best food, moving around the garden throughout the day to catch the sun, finding the softest, most comfortable places to lie.

They are resourceful, too. When they don't find enough food from willing islanders, they investigate the garbage sacks left out for collection. To discourage the cats from tearing open the bags, some residents hang the garbage sacks from their fences or gates. But these become even more tempting and are treated as feline *piñatas*. The cats amuse themselves by taking swipes at the swinging bags, then wait for the food to spill out for easy dining.

******

The animals are an integral part of island life, from the beauty of a line of seagulls in the sky to the clumsy antics of stray kittens. But the special character of the island's animals is their unnatural willingness to coexist peacefully.

We see young seagulls walking along the island streets, unable to fly back to the nest, trying to find familiar territory. They may walk past cats, within inches of dogs, all of them observed by one or more crows. They all ignore each other. The dogs never think of chasing the cats; the cats have minimal interest in scaring the birds. It seems impossible and yet it is the island way.

I can only think it is somehow an echo of the island's long history of tolerance. Dogs and cats, cats and birds, Muslims and Christians, Greeks and Turks...on Heybeliada, all seem to be unaware that elsewhere they are expected to be natural enemies.

XXII
OTHER PLANS

Life is what happens to you while you're busy making other plans.
John Lennon

Have you ever noticed that most books about moving to a foreign country cover only the settling-in period? There's a fairy tale quality about them: I quit my boring job, moved to a place of sunshine and mandolins, and lived happily ever after.

In fact, once the reality sinks in, many people find that they miss the stimulation and just plain human contact they had in their jobs. They decide that their charming village or mountaintop isn't really entertaining enough to fill up 24 hours a day, 365 days a year. So they move on.

There's less risk of that on Heybeliada, where Istanbul is within easy reach. With apologies to Samuel Johnson, "She who is tired of Istanbul is tired of life." For the first few years on the island, before I retired and while Ben was still teaching, these questions didn't arise. We had more than enough to fill our time, and if we couldn't get back to the island easily at night, we had a Bosphorus-view apartment that came with my job.

Finally, we took the plunge with early retirement. Admittedly, there is a period of sheer ecstasy when you've first shaken off a demanding job. Idleness feels wonderful. In the first month after my retirement, my leisurely mornings always included listening to radio reports of commuter traffic jams in the metropolitan area. I just sipped my coffee and relished the *schadenfreude*.

But nevertheless I plead guilty. I soon found myself wondering "what next?" Our generation seems to be reinventing retirement as a time to do and try things we didn't have time for while working full-time. Retirement no longer means sitting in a rocking chair or riding a golf cart all day. With no job demands to hold us, we could shape our time however we liked.

Before long, however, our time began to shape itself. The first turning point was during an evening with Uğur and Inci at the home of a mutual friend. The food was excellent, and the conversation lively. Then our host asked Uğur, who had already written several guides to Turkey in Turkish, what he was currently working on.

"My life's dream." he replied. "I want to write a comprehensive guide to Turkey in English, illustrated with my own photos, but I need help. My English needs a lot of polishing, so I have to find an editor."

I heard someone saying, "Perfect. I have plenty of free time, have a lot of editing experience, and would be glad to help you." Then I realized the voice was mine.

Uğur and I worked together on his book over several weeks, polishing and rewriting until we were both sure this was a book we could be proud of. One way and another, I'd done a lot of editing over the years and enjoyed doing it, but had never thought of it as a career. Now I began to see this as a possible part-time option in retirement.

About the same time, we began to think that a full 12-month island life might not be for us. Along with no job demands, there was also no job-related apartment in the city, no place to retreat to in deepest winter, when the weather turns nasty and the islands are thinly populated. As a native San Franciscan, I've never been a fan of winter weather. A good retirement goal, I thought, might be to avoid ever seeing snow again.

Kısmet stepped in again. We began to consider spending part of the winter in San Francisco—my hometown, the city where Ben and I first met, and a fine place to avoid snow. When I discovered that I could do a professional editing course there, we considered it more seriously. About the same time, an American university decided to establish new programs in Turkey and asked us to help them as consultants. Could we come to them, visit the interested campuses, and talk about how they should proceed?

That tipped the balance. A little time each winter in the United States would lead to new ways to be involved in Turkish life through publishing and academia. A win-win option.

I was delighted to return to San Francisco. Although we had spent many years overseas, I always considered myself a San Franciscan at heart. I think my initial fondness for Istanbul might have been influenced by certain similarities to San Francisco: hills, sea, bridges, seagulls, even earthquakes. But we found that San Francisco had changed as a result of the dot-com boom and, when we first settled there, we knew only a couple of old school friends. I wondered if today's Bay Area residents would all turn out to be like the Montessori Mom from Marin County who had blighted that evening at our favorite *meyhane*.

There were many unexpected culture shocks, but, finally, we adjusted, found new friends, and experienced what I call the Belma Principle. Belma, our friend in the pickle village of Çengelköy, spends her winters in London. The Belma Principle states that whichever of the two homes you are in, you can't imagine why you would ever return to the other. When, in fact, you return, you wonder why you waited so long and can't imagine going back to the other. She was quite right. We have now settled into a fine pattern of living both places and loving both of them. But I now realize that my renewed love for San Francisco is not based on the fact that it's my hometown or that it combines wonderful climate with the country's best food and wine. No, I realized, just as I first loved Istanbul because it reminded me of San Francisco, the tables have turned. Looking at the San Francisco skyline now makes me think of Istanbul. Josephine Baker would understand: her song *"J'ai deux amours, mon pays et Paris"* needs only the substitution of Istanbul for Paris.

But in the United States, we also discovered part of the reason for many people's reluctance to come to Turkey. Americans get very little international news, and most of what they get about Turkey is bad. Even we, who should know better, begin to wonder if things have gone awry, if we should reconsider the idea of returning to Istanbul. But when we return, we again wonder why we ever left our island, even for a few weeks.

This necklace of green islands adorning the Sea of Marmara may seem removed from the rest of the world, particularly in the winter season, but, of course, as part of Istanbul, the archipelago also lives in the 21st century with the good and the bad that comes with that. Is Heybeliada an earthly paradise? No, of course not. On the island, in Istanbul, in Turkey, there are frustrating moments, incomprehensible events, thorny political and economic issues, a full range of human failings, and the usual array of troublesome problems and human tragedies that are part of daily life anywhere in the world.

Mother Nature also throws natural disasters in Turkey's path. In August 1999, a 7.4 magnitude earthquake struck Izmit, about fifty miles southeast of Istanbul but close enough to rattle the city and cause serious damage in outlying areas. Buildings crumbled. Thousands died. Newspaper reports noted that another fault lies under the Sea of Marmara, not far from the Princes' Islands. Many people panicked and said they would not return to the islands, "due" for a Big One since the last major quake was in 1894.

Calmer heads point out that the islands are solid rock and the older wooden houses have the necessary "give" to ride with a temblor. For a few seasons after the 1999 disaster, the islands' summer population declined dramatically, but within five years, the crowds were back again. As the earthquake memories fade, more Istanbul residents are finding it attractive to escape their long and frustrating car commutes by living on the islands, spending their travel time reading the newspaper and sipping tea aboard one of the graceful ferryboats to the mainland.

How long will Ben and I stay here? Who knows? Maybe forever, maybe not. The time we spend in San Francisco is a comfortable interlude and a nice change of scene, but for now it is Turkey that feels more like home. Nonetheless, we are aware that the island's magic is fragile. The balance of tradition and modernity could too easily be tipped, turning Heybeliada into just another Istanbul district with no special character of its own.

Change is inevitable, of course. San Francisco is not the place it was when I was growing up, but it is still the only place I can imagine living in the United States. The island, too, is changing. We hear complaints from longtime islanders, but I heard the same complaints when I first came to the island house and met the complaining old woman, Nuray Hanım, on the ferryboat. Nostalgia for the old days and ways continues to be an island tradition.

We asked Turkish friends and other expatriates what they think about the worries and dire predictions of various Cassandras who are convinced that Turkey is headed for disaster. Some echoed concerns about religious-secular tensions; some worried about economic indicators; others predicted upheaval if Turkey's EU bid is rejected.

But today, as in Atatürk's time, Turkey's young population is the hope for the future, and bright young students, whatever their family background, can gain social mobility through their own talent and effort. Some of the young people are impatient with efforts to deal with today's problems. They complain of too few university places and jobs for too many talented young people; too much corruption in government or business; too many obstacles in the way of ambitious entrepreneurs; or not enough haste in making needed reforms. When I asked some Turkish university students what they saw as the three biggest challenges facing Turkey in the next decades, not a single one mentioned the Islam-secular divide. Their concerns were an echo of Bill Clinton's "It's the economy, stupid." They are bright, well educated, and eager. Give me a chance, they say, and I can do anything. Turkish young people are making their world marks in everything from computer science to filmmaking to international finance. The Turkish Republic has come a long way in its 80+ years, with the tempo of change increasing after the economic reforms of the 1980s. Today, the dynamism of the young people and the pace of Turkey's development are powerful and positive indicators for its future. Despite some Turkish alarmists who see change as threat, I am convinced that Turkey has a very bright future. Time will tell whether or not I am too optimistic.

But for now, this remains one of the most satisfying places I could imagine living. Every year, on October 29, the anniversary of the Turkish republic, we raise a glass of *rakı* in honor of Atatürk and the Turkish people, and especially Turkey's youth. By a stroke of *kısmet,* that day is also Ben's birthday. And it is often one of the last nice days before winter begins to set in.

Taking all into account, life in Turkey, in Istanbul, on Heybeliada, seems to me about as good as it gets. And what about that Istanbul earthquake that is "due"? As a San Franciscan, I don't fret about possible earthquakes. If it comes, it comes. If it's part of the *kısmet* of the place, so be it.

Meanwhile, I intend to focus on another k-word: *keyif*. It means a feeling of pleasure in life, of delight and well-being. It may have been *kısmet* that brought us here, but it is *keyif* that keeps us here—the delight in the rhythm and variety of life, the frisson of exquisite moments like the silent sunset departure of the storks, the warmth and depth of the friendships we have experienced here, the intellectual stimulation of a society rediscovering its past while building its future, the double pleasure of a tranquil retreat with an exciting city just moments away.

Spring is my favorite season on the island, the time when Heybeliada emerges from its winter cocoon and begins preparations for the summer onslaught. Roads are repaired, novice ferry personnel practice docking the boats efficiently, notices are posted for recruiting new *fayton* drivers. The first of the summer residents appear on weekends to begin checking on their houses and arranging for spring-cleaning. There is a feeling of renewal and rebirth.

April 23 is a Turkish holiday in honor of "children and national sovereignty." That may seem an odd holiday combination until you realize that it is, in fact, a day of homage to Atatürk's legacy: to the importance he attached to youth in his new nation, and to the anniversary of the first parliament of the Turkish republic. Each April 23, a parade along the Heybeliada seafront ends at the statue of Atatürk, which is inscribed with his famous words, "Happy is the one who can say 'I am a Turk.'" On Children's Day, all the local worthies have a chance to speak: the island's *muhtar* (district administrator), the school principal, some of the teachers. Children in school uniforms recite poems in the stentorian style they are taught to use. Others sing an *a cappella* version of the Turkish national anthem. The smallest girls, in traditional costumes, perform folk dances.

Children's Day is a big event throughout the country, but on these islands—with their *Rum* heritage—April 23 is also celebrated as the feast of St. George. Hordes of pilgrims and tourists, Muslim as well as Christian, come to the islands' monasteries for the year's most sacred Greek Orthodox ceremonies. The largest group of pilgrims, on Büyükada, will walk—some of them on their knees—up the highest hill to the monastery of St. George, while Turkish children participate in the national festivities at the water's edge.

It is a one-day survey of island—or even Istanbul—history: the Byzantine and Greek Orthodox heritage, the Ottoman past, and the vitality of the 80+-year-old secular Turkish republic. It is also a overview of today's Turks: earnest young students in school uniforms, government officials in suits, parents and other spectators in everything from village garb to high fashion, laborers in caps and work clothes, Greek Orthodox priests in long black robes, residents and visitors from a multitude of ethnic backgrounds. Ever-larger crowds of Greek visitors appear on the islands for Easter or the feast of St. George and are viewed by the locals as a first indication of the coming tourist season. Will this be a good year? Or will world events once again dampen enthusiasm for travel to this part of the world?

In summer, when the islands are most crowded, *keyif* comes from outdoor evenings with friends, the bountiful and changing flowers, the sparkle of the sun on water morphing from powder blue to teal green and, yes, even "wine dark" at stormy times. As fall approaches, winter's repose is heralded by the departure of the storks and of the summer residents.

The island winter can be difficult. The summerhouses, even when heated, are never quite warm enough. The weekly market shrinks to a few shivering merchants with limited wares. Other services become scarcer. Many of our friends return to their city homes for easier commute to work or because of their children's school needs. The ferry schedule is reduced and boats are cancelled during the worst of the *lodos* winds. But even with these drawbacks, the stillness and emptiness of the island's winter months have their own beauty and provide another side of *keyif*. This is what Lawrence Durrell, writing about the island of Cyprus, described as "the contemplation which comes of silence and ease." Winter *keyif* is not for everyone. The island, now devoid of crowds, offers a simpler existence, uninterrupted by the demands of everyday city life. The silence of the island deepens, the colors shift to more melancholic shades, but for some islanders, winter is the secret treasure, bringing the deeper *keyif* that conjures up visions of the island's long ago past. It is possible to imagine how content those Byzantine monks might have been.

No season is complete in itself, and the modern islander is no monk. But the changing nature of the island keeps the experience of living here fresh. And, as always, one of the world's most exciting cities is within view and easy reach. *Keyif* can take on different attributes in each season, and another description of *keyif* is "a state of suspended judgment." We indulge in this form of *keyif* as well, savoring both the island life and the brief interlude in California, refusing to worry about what may or may not come to pass in the future. But most of all, our *keyif* is just the daily joy of being in Turkey among the Turks. Especially on an island in Istanbul.

About the Author

M.A. Whitten first came to Turkey in the 1970s as a university lecturer and has maintained her connection to the country ever since. At various times, she has worked in Turkey as a teacher, diplomat, editor, and consultant. She currently divides her time between San Francisco and Istanbul. This is her first book.